Where are the fish?
Where is the fish story?

First things first! You can not read a book and fish at the same time, lest the fish are not biting. Right?

Timing is everything.
Well, let's read now and fish later.

We will be covering an aeronautical flight "R&D" procedure inside Unknown Physics. This is a threshold reading opportunity for all ages, especially here in the
First in Flight state of North Carolina.

I have asked our U. S. Armed Forces to start "R&D" programs with a star-burst/wagon-wheel walk through light weight frame; supplemented with public input from NASA and physics departments nation wide.

This is a public presentation expected to become an active U. S. Armed Forces enlistment reality.

However; an argument seems to be engaging between some Star Wars realist expressing the need for the entire Pentagon "R&D" funding budget going to real warfare first and only. Forgive me for arguing for Peace and say: "Yes", for the public computer based Project: "Good Karma" "R&D". Think of North Carolina's Universities and North Carolina's Colleges.
Then think of NATO and beyond.

All that education for the cost of one

Aeronautical Engineering Computer
That is a good business plan !!!!

Variables

The variables specific to Project: "Good Karma" are the space needed to house this unknown technology and the weight of that unknown technology between our wing-blades and frame. We will have to design new applications for known technology in an almost opposite alignment of the known technology used in our contemporary jet engines. This state of "Does not exist as yet." is not an obstacle. It is an inspiration to achieve this unknown technology with the help of a public NASA based Aeronautical Engineering Computer. "Impossible" is not acceptable in a world that has toured our universe with known technology. The fact that this new aeronautical design is not a military advantage in its present form is not a civilian disadvantage. However, many if not all adverse findings while developing such electro magnetic field transfer R&D could be used for a military advantage by outside national military interests. But, PEACE is our technological objective right alongside contemporary flight in the likeness of our universe. Farming incoming meteorites is our extended international non-nuclear application of this new technology.

Any and all micro or macro alternative applications of magnetic bearings, maglev technology, metallurgy, electro magnetic transfer, etc. will be studied under our USA National Security interests. An international participation is anticipated. The normal "Top Secret" stigma binding standard national security oversight vs a public "R&D" inside unknown technology is an active reality. This NASA based Aeronautical Engineering Computer offering a secondary window for advanced public education input is not the same as Wilber and Orville Write becoming the First in Flight in 1903. The difference is a stronger NATO and USA. Say "Yes" and be a voice for Team USA.

Project: "Good Karma"

A publicly presented Nuclear Disarmament Program to build an aircraft/spacecraft designed after our very own

Milky Way Universe

Building our USA Team
<Go-Fund-Me>

Author: Nick Webster
Free Agent SNW ~ License Pending
DOB: 08~06~1946, Boston
400 Money Island Drive
Atlantic Beach, North Carolina 28512
Nickwebster1946@outlook.com
970-946-3858

Briefing Phase III:

April 6th, 2018; marking our 1st Year.

NASA and our United States Armed Forces
have received Project: "Good Karma" as should be our first
objective. Phase **III** involves public participation.
This phase seeks grant development for students here in
North Carolina, Carteret Community College, other colleges,
and other universities, as with industrial participation.

To do that and more Phase **III** expands public awareness.
Public awareness and public opinion on a national level
will determine our future as
Project: "Good Karma".

We can work together in the spirit of NASA and
Captain Michael Smith of Beaufort, N. C.
Captain Michael Smith was born April 30, 1945.
Captain Smith tragically perished with the entire crew of the
Challenger Mission spacecraft's departure take-off from
Kennedy Space Center on January 28th, 1986.

Project: Good Karma wants to reside beside Eagleworks of Johnson Space Center, NASA, in Houston where Dr. Harold "Sonny" White is publicly developing an unknown physics formulary for Warp Speed. This NASA based public physics formulary class for the study of Warp Speed is a key intellectual objective giving support for the study of Project: "Good Karma"; also a study in unknown physics.

Basically the macro application of the warp speed formulary is for space travel outside our atmosphere. While the micro application of such physics will work well for the here and now Project: Good Karma's self generating electric fuel sustaining flight inside our atmosphere.

Now you know why all this comes down to a good days fishing on the Oceanana Pier.

Everybody knows talking about the here and now makes for a good day's fishing.

Yes, talking about the Project: "Good Karma" aircraft/spacecraft is the first line of support to see this First in Flight mission gets the attention it needs.

Project: "Good Karma" needs you in the big picture.

Project: "Good Karma"
Phase III "R&D"
Requested NASA Computer Based "R&D" Objectives

1st: Design a Computer Based Frame. I have submitted my frame design within Phase I. This provides a cost efficient study of a basic flight ready frame ready for improvements. Easy to adapt ideas at the designer end without material expenses; Eng. Rms./Observation Areas/Frame.

2nd: Design a Computer Based Drive-beam. I have submitted several Drive-beam designs in Phase I. Wing-blades A, B, & C to be powered to 30,000 RPMs {+ or -}. The drive-beam function is to ride within the maglev process and to thereby lift the aircraft/spacecraft into sustained flight. The round/tubular drive-beam; as is shown in Phase I is technologically more difficult to manufacture/produce than a flat against flat maglev surface forged in a circular framework for "R&D" purposes. Therefore, we can start our "R&D" computer based drive beam and maglev contact areas with flat 6 to 10 inch contact areas; three such contact areas to each side of each wing-blade maglev area.

3rd: Standardize all materials specific to the moving parts of a contemporary jet engine towards the new configuration of like/same function needed for flight reality with Project: "Good Karma". I seek professional engineers to properly design a contemporary tricentric generator inside a tricentric aircraft/spacecraft or 9-planet design aircraft/spacecraft as introduced in Phase I. I seek grants to all physics departments in every college and university in our entire U. S. of A.

Entering Unknown Physics:

Basically I started by designing a flying generator powered by a helicopter engine. I then knowingly burdened that helicopter engine with more than it was intended to do. That start-up is not expected to fly. However, it may fly. As we power our maglev bearings we decrease the burden of tribology. As we generate enough electricity to feed our electric overdrive we again increase our RPMs, lessen the known burden of tribology, and we turn off that helicopter engine. Our long term goal to become self powering/self sufficient; equilibrium of mechanical motion in flight powered by internally produced electricity is nearing completion. There and then we feed our ultimate flight goal of an internal electric laser propulsion overdrive to the drive-beam itself; an unknown process. There and then we program a desired 30,000 RPMs {+ or -} for VTO and sustained flight.

I first thought helicopter start-up. I then thought multiple fan jets would be more appropriate for this project. NASA may think nuclear start-up.

Advanced Computer Flight Probability Studies:
Yes, a contemporary fan jet arrangement; as shown in Phase I will work well for this maglev stage and sustaining flight RPMs.

Internally generated electricity will sustain flight. I bring the helicopter engine into consideration as a primary start-up power source; for computer based flight consideration because the traditional helicopter engine is a VTO workhorse. However, the body/work weight is much less than our proposed "Flying Generator". However, the missing known technology needed is made obvious; in ratios. Our first solution must center on our maglev bearing technology and our internal ability to generate the needed electricity to activate those maglev bearings.

At that standard the jet fueled helicopter/fan jet/etc engine shuts off; as the regeneration of needed electricity is reached.

That ratio of electrical regeneration capability with application to maglev bearings and main drive beam over-drive is unknown today. So also is the NASA formulary for Warp Speed unknown. NASA's Johnson Space Center has entered a public Physics standard vocabulary explaining the terms unto comprehensively reaching the yet unknown accomplishment of a man-made spacecraft exiting our universe at Warp Speed. There-in; this unknown and developing formulary for Warp Speed, is food for thought while focusing on Project: "Good Karma". Project: "Good Karma" chooses to stay Earth bound.

Both projects can exchange and interchange the goal of mega distance. Eagleworks @ JSC chooses distance @ warp speed from and return to our Milky Way Universe. Project: "Good Karma" chooses short earthly distances achieved via the regeneration of electric fuel generated by weight displacement in mechanized motion at contemporary flight speeds. Perhaps Project: "Good Karma" will also reach an unknown warp speed here on earth; perhaps. We; both projects, seek unknown technology. Project: "Good Karma" seeks the ability to regenerate our electric feed that stabilizes both our maglev bearings and laser driven over-drive flight RPMs. Again that RPM standard for electric feed regeneration is also an unknown today. Phase III is now @ your finger tips. This Phase III of Project: "Good Karma" hopes to gain the financial support to reside under the NASA umbrella. Project: "Good Karma" seeks to become a public/corporate study like Eagleworks of Johnson Space Center, NASA. I have asked to join the NASA team in Cape Canaveral, California, or Colorado.

Google >>> Eagleworks, JSC; Johnson Space Center <<< for NASA's ongoing study of Warp Speed and related physics still unknown just like Project: "Good Karma"..

The rest is history in the making. See you there.

Project: "Good Karma"

Two Boats School
School Project

Project: "Good Karma" centers on International Technology Sharing and International Nuclear Disarmament via a "R&D" aviation project; building an aircraft designed after our very own Milky Way Universe. Captain S.N. Webster designed and patented the start-up aircraft/spacecraft back in the 80's and 90's. Today's graphics depict a futuristic evolution from the original patented aircraft/spacecraft, as you will see. Bringing an "R&D" project revolving around a requested NASA computer based "R&D" Flight Probability Analysis is a bold undertaking for my Two Boats School; a Sea of Math home-schooling program. I started this home-schooling program because earning a living on the Sea was and is a great honor. Meeting my maker face to wind and wave was and is the greatest honor I know. For those reasons I now share the Laws of the Sea, the Sea of Math, and the aircraft/spacecraft represented in Project "Good Karma". Again, Project: "Good Karma" is our school project because I needed to do my intellectual best in overcoming what I saw as an Eternal War behind us.

About the aircraft/spacecraft; when NASA completes their computer based Flight Probability Analysis we will all know what our best in NASA know about Project: "Good Karma".

This is how Project: "Good Karma" took form on April 6th, 2017.

Project: "Good Karma"

An International Technology Sharing
"Research & Development" Project
to build an aircraft designed after our own

Milky Way Universe

FIG. 5-A

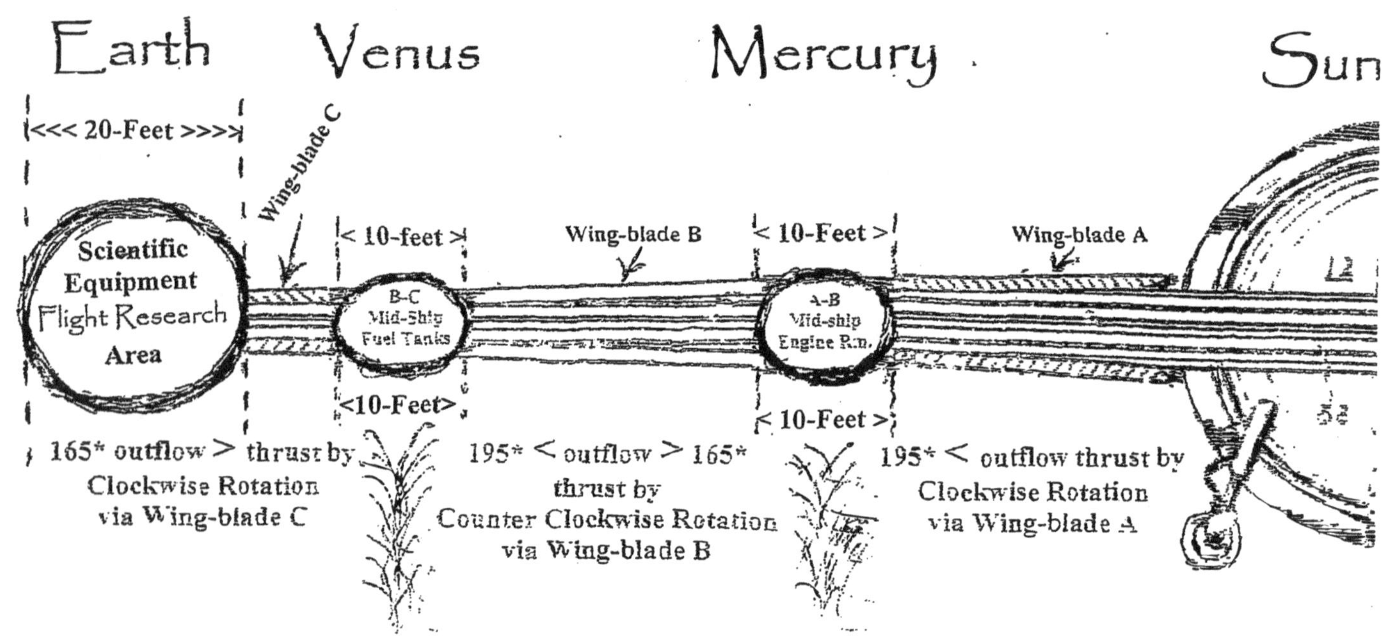

The above references to 165-Degrees & 195 Degrees
are by Solar North as if the Sun at high noon were North.

Up-dated March 5th, 2017 offering of now outdated patents
U.S. Patent 5,213,284; 5/25/93 & Design Patent 320,378; 10/01/91
by S. N. Webster, DOB 08/06/1946, Boston

Briefing:

On April 06, 2017 Senator Bill Nelson
forwarded Project: "Good Karma" to NASA
for a computer flight probability analysis.

On April 26th, 2017: Pratt & Whitney
expressed regret that they will not be participating
in international technology sharing through
Project: "Good Karma".

The following is that Phase I presentation.

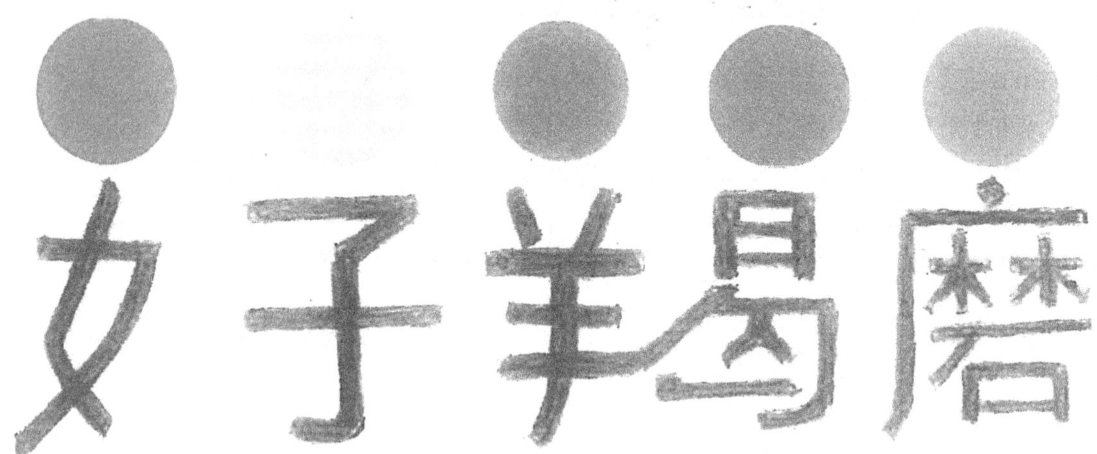

Project: "Good Karma"

Hǎo jiémó

总统 President Donald Trump

And

总统 President Xi Jinping

Presented for tabling during the
Meeting Of Presidents; April 6th, 2017

Prepared by: SNWebster

Page #5
Project: "Good Karma"

11

To the:

Honorable United States President Donald Trump
and
Honorable Chinese President Xi Jinping

Sirs, I thank my Honorable Senator Bill Nelson for bringing this Project: "Good Karma" before you at this time. I wish to inspire children and adults alike to dream, study, and overcome "Eternal War". The aircraft documentation introduced here-in seemingly separates my humble beginnings with paper and pen from completion with the term { **Expired** }. Project: "Good Karma" can be completed without my oversight. I simply offer my support for the completion of Project: "Good Karma" at this time via this meeting of our
United States President Trump and Chinese President Jinping.

To my corresponding Chinese team,

Your maglev technology is big thunder. I do not yet understand everything you have done. Congratulations! I ask you. Can you make this now out-dated by patent coverage; VAu 48-797, mobile wing tricentric displacement aircraft fly with your maglev technology? I can only imagine how. Our countries and peoples should technologically evolve together.

Respectfully yours in Christ @ Sea & @ Home.
With Peace of Mind.

Steven Nichols Webster
Steven Nichols Webster

Project: "Good Karma"

April 03, 2017

Purpose: USA/China Technology Sharing

Program: Research & Development, Aviation

Objective: Build an aircraft designed after our very own universe the Milky Way by width and depth.

Reason: To build a "Vehicle of Peace" in thought, word, and deed; ownership investment by participating nations. "All Nations Invited."

History: November 15, 1989

I; S. N. Webster, authored a USA/USSR Nuclear Disarmament Proposal Counter Atomic Attack System One; Operation: Cultivation of the Stars. There-in I offered the original patents that this Project: "Good Karma" is centered on as the mission aircraft. CAASO; Op: CS was a predecessor to the International Space Station we know today. Today, Chinese maglev bearings may just be the technology needed to get Project: "Good Karma" off the ground.

by   S. N. Webster

Patent Up-Date Continuance Pending
Official USA Corporate/Government Participation
Request Drafted: March 05, 2017

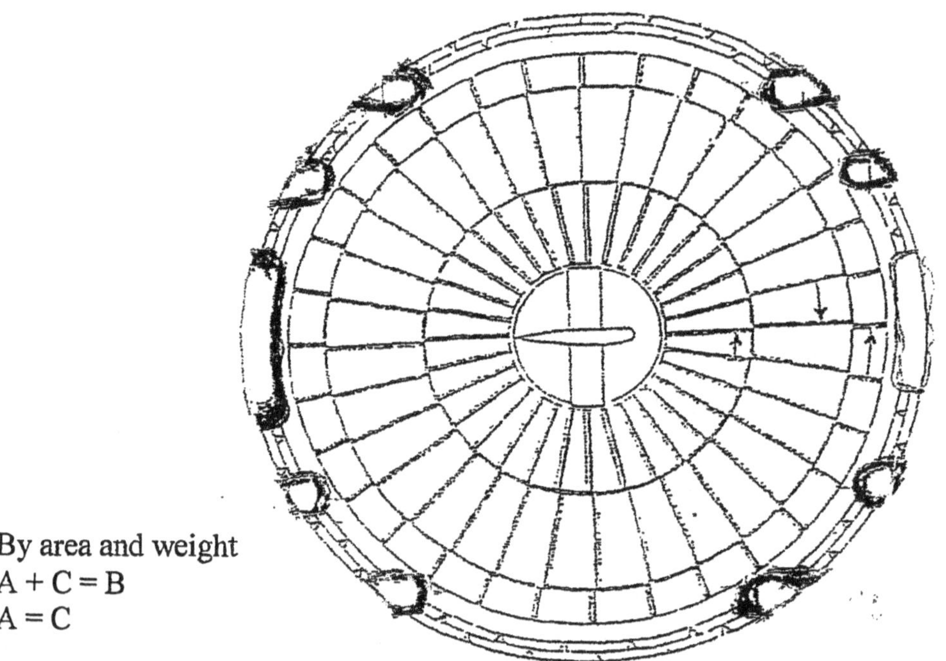

By area and weight
A + C = B
A = C

By area only
A + B + C = 80% r6

By width only
d = e
r6 + 2d = r7
r6 + 2e = r7

FIG. 3 - A

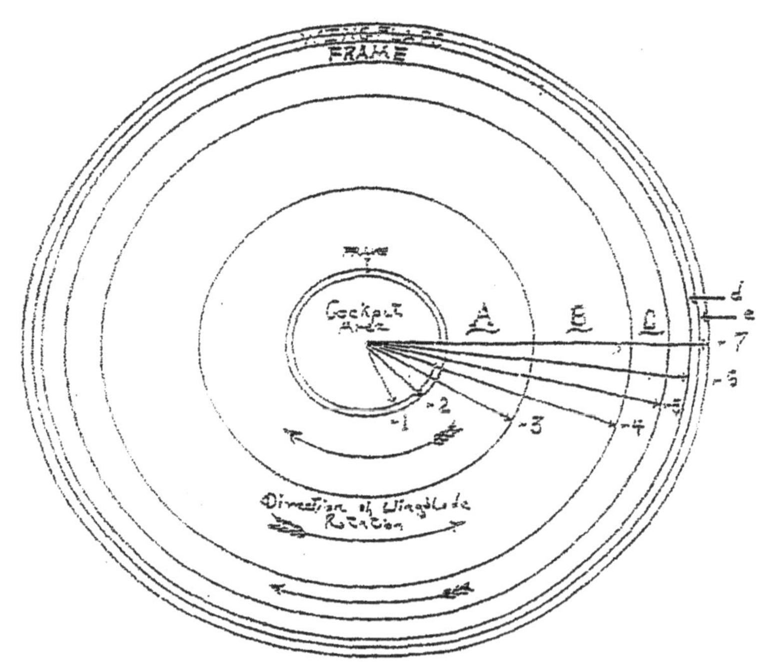

FIG. 3 - B

Page #8
Project: "Good Karma"

Patent Up-Date Continuance Pending
Official USA Corporate/Government Participation
Request Drafted: March 05, 2017

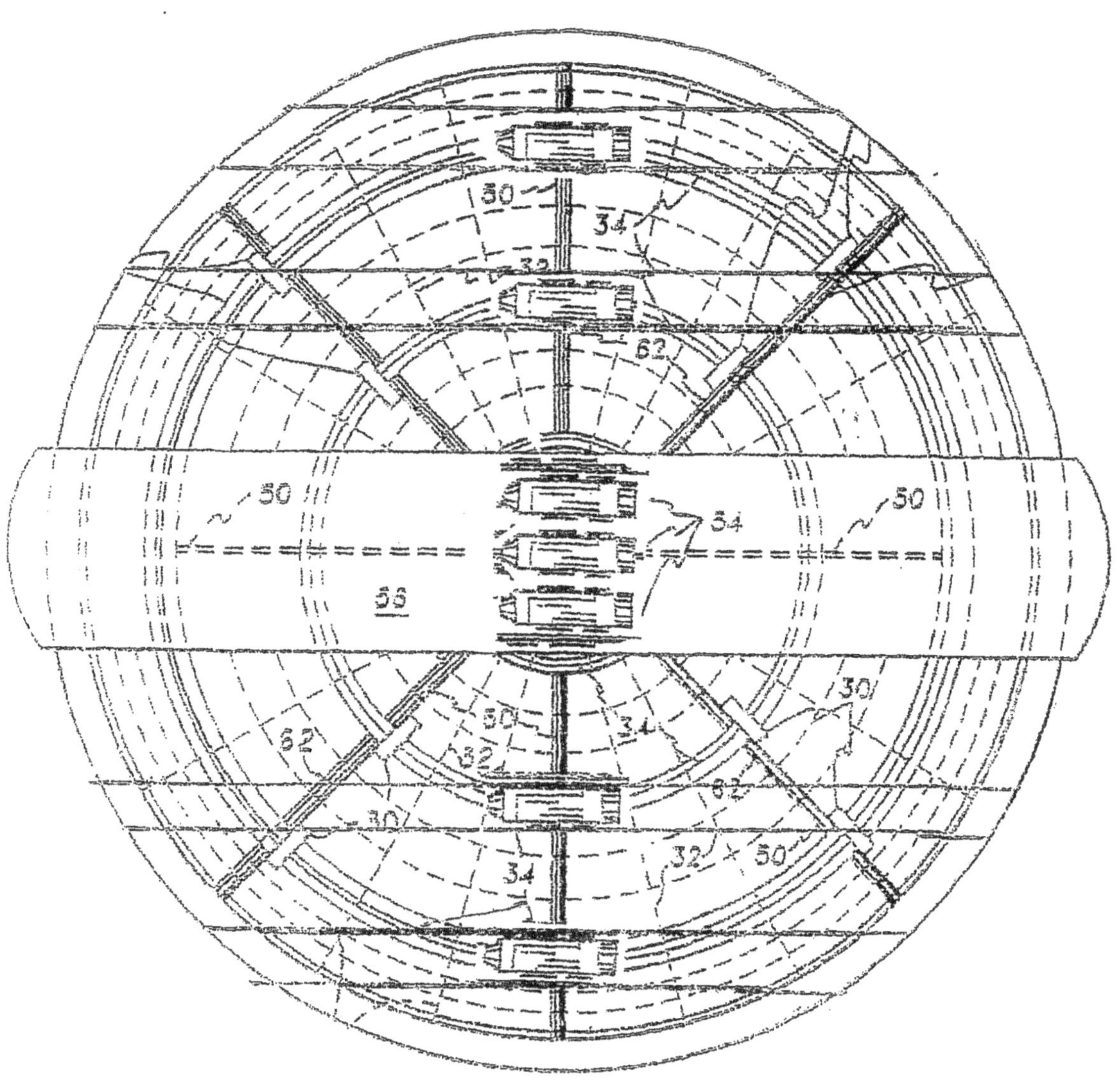

FIG. 4 -A

Patent Up-Date Continuance Pending
Official USA Corporate/Government Participation
Request Drafted: March 05, 2017

FIG. 5-A

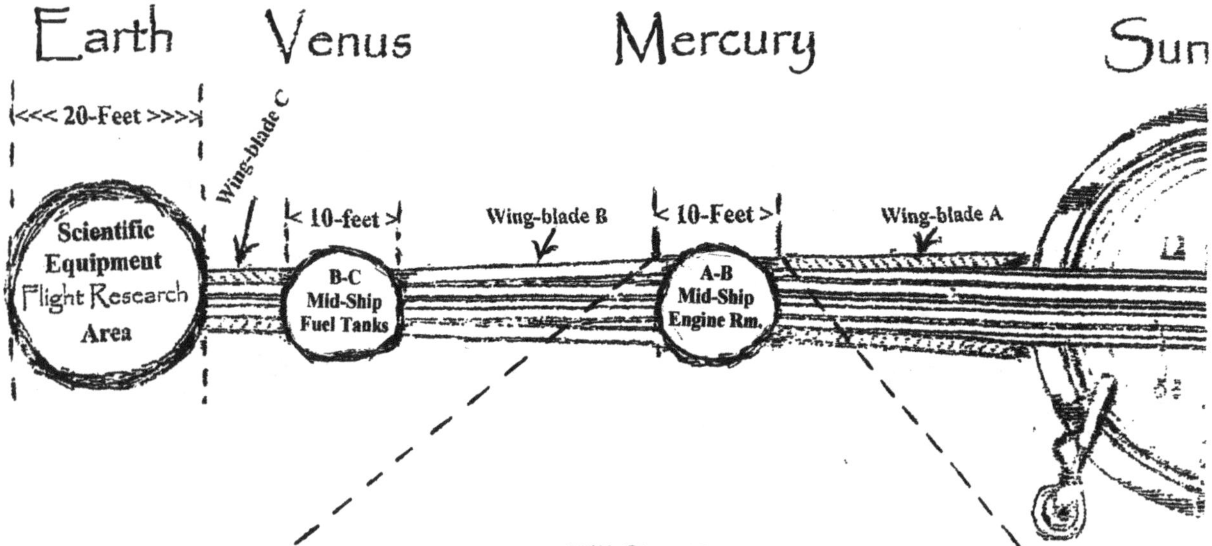

FIG. 7-A

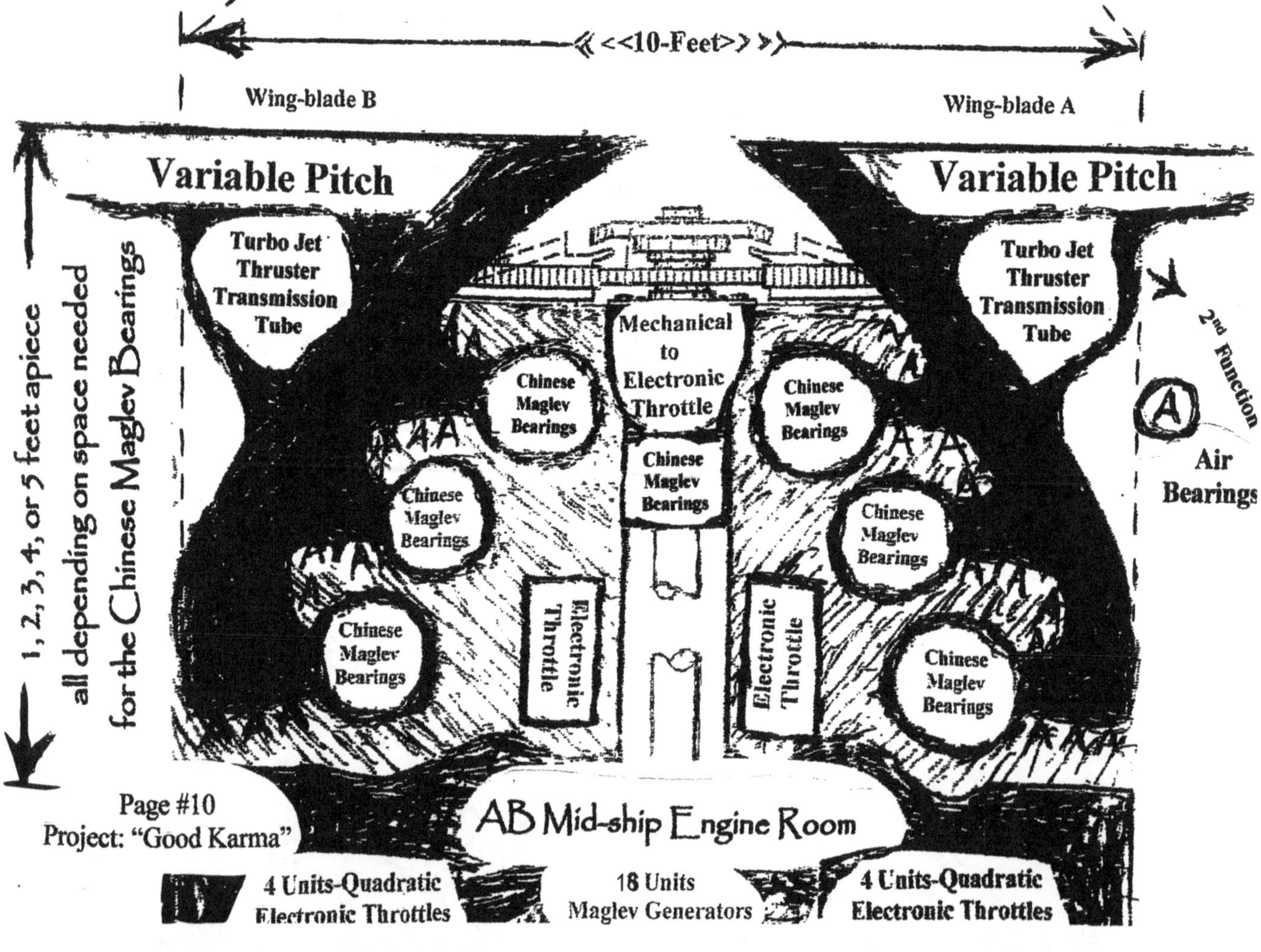

Page #10
Project: "Good Karma"

Patent Up-Date Continuance Pending
Official USA Corporate/Government Participation
Request Drafted: March 05, 2017

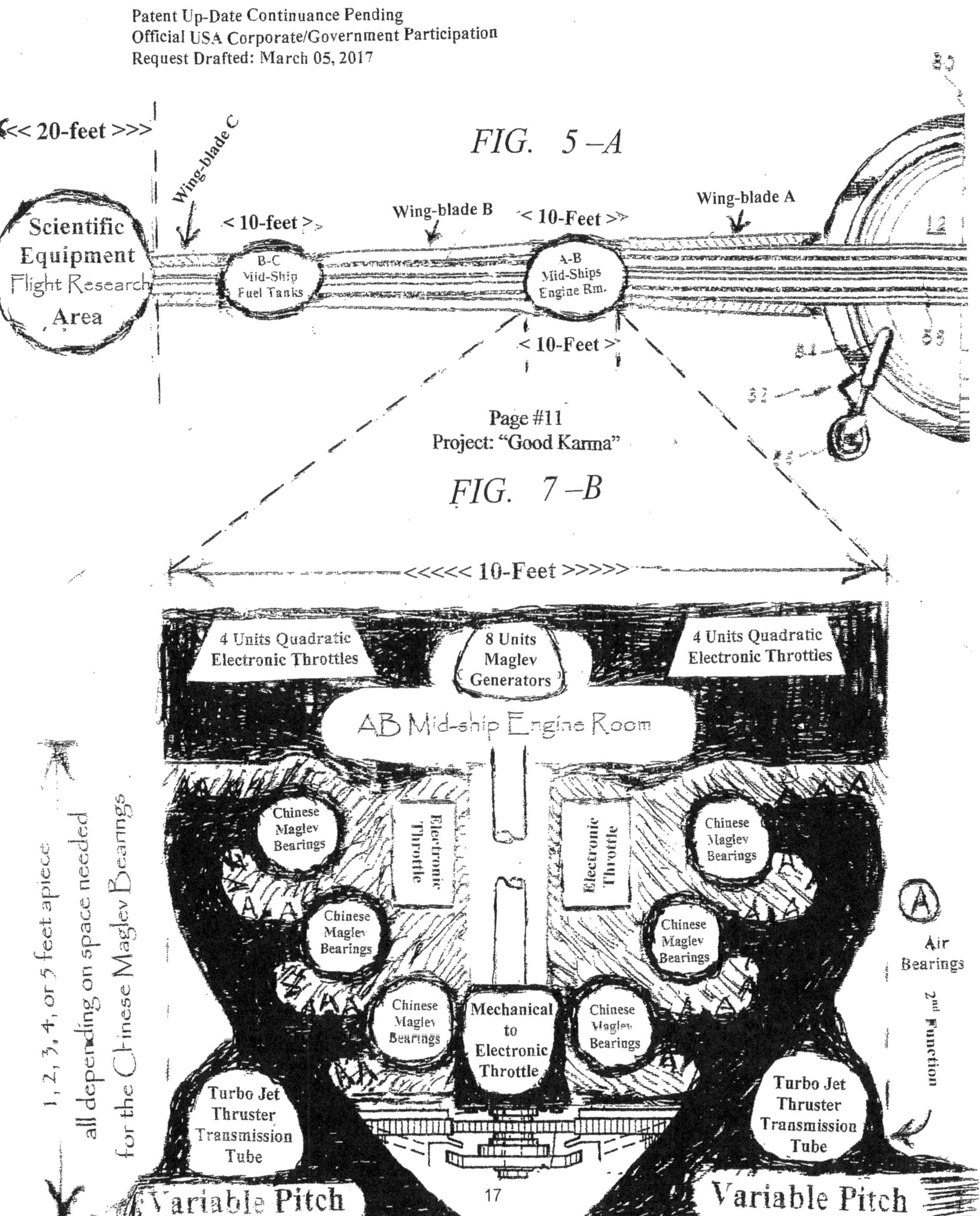

Patent Up-Date Continuance Pending Participation
Official USA Corporate/Government
Request Drafted: March 05, 2017

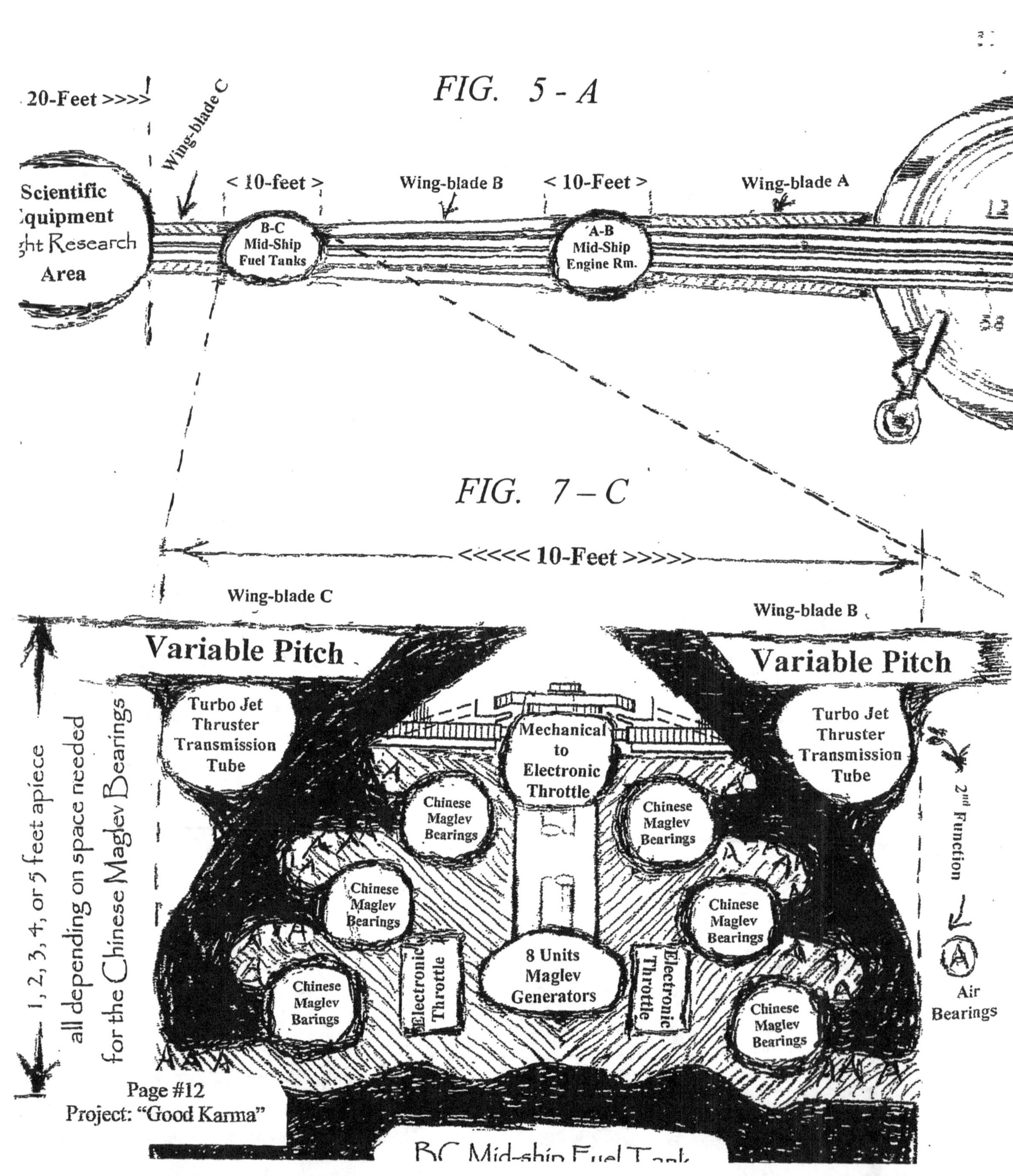

Patent Up-Date Continuance Pending Participation
Official USA Corporate/Government
Request Drafted: March 05, 2017

FIG. 5 - A

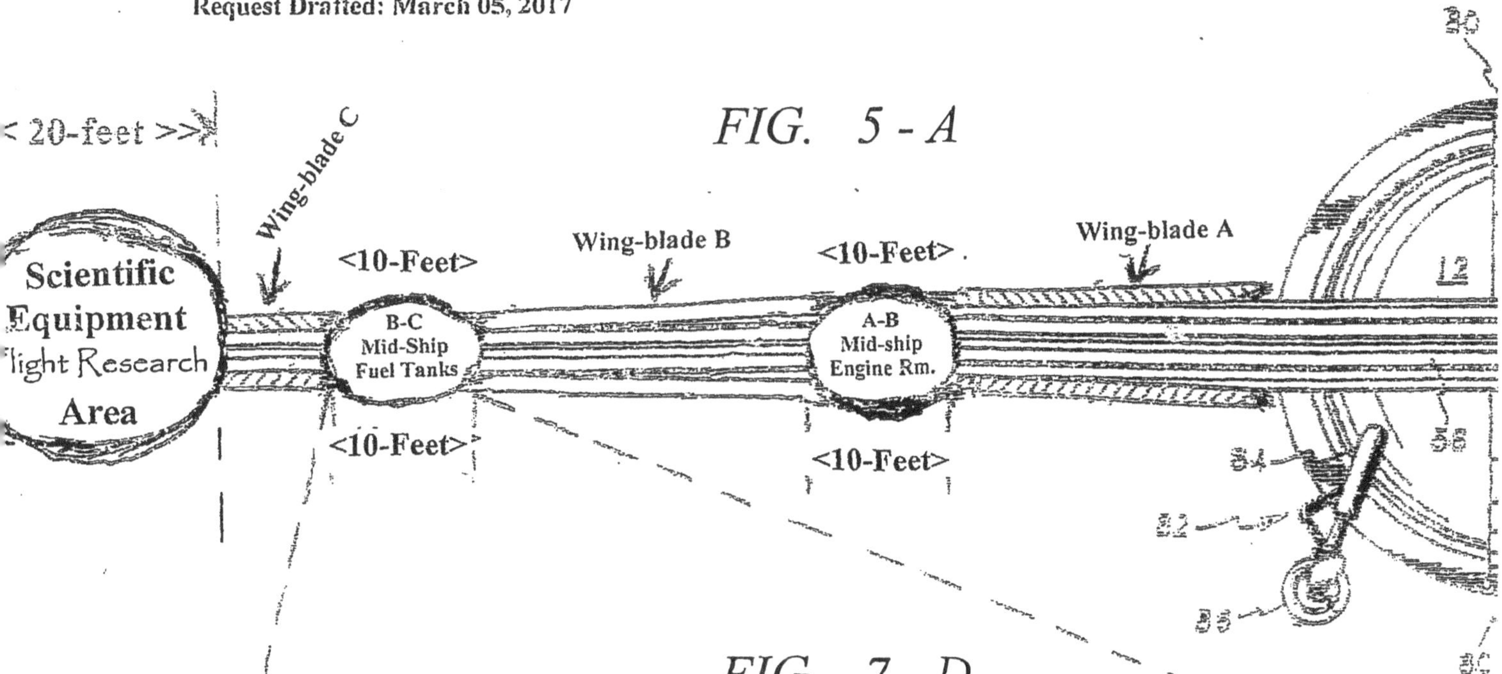

FIG. 7 - D

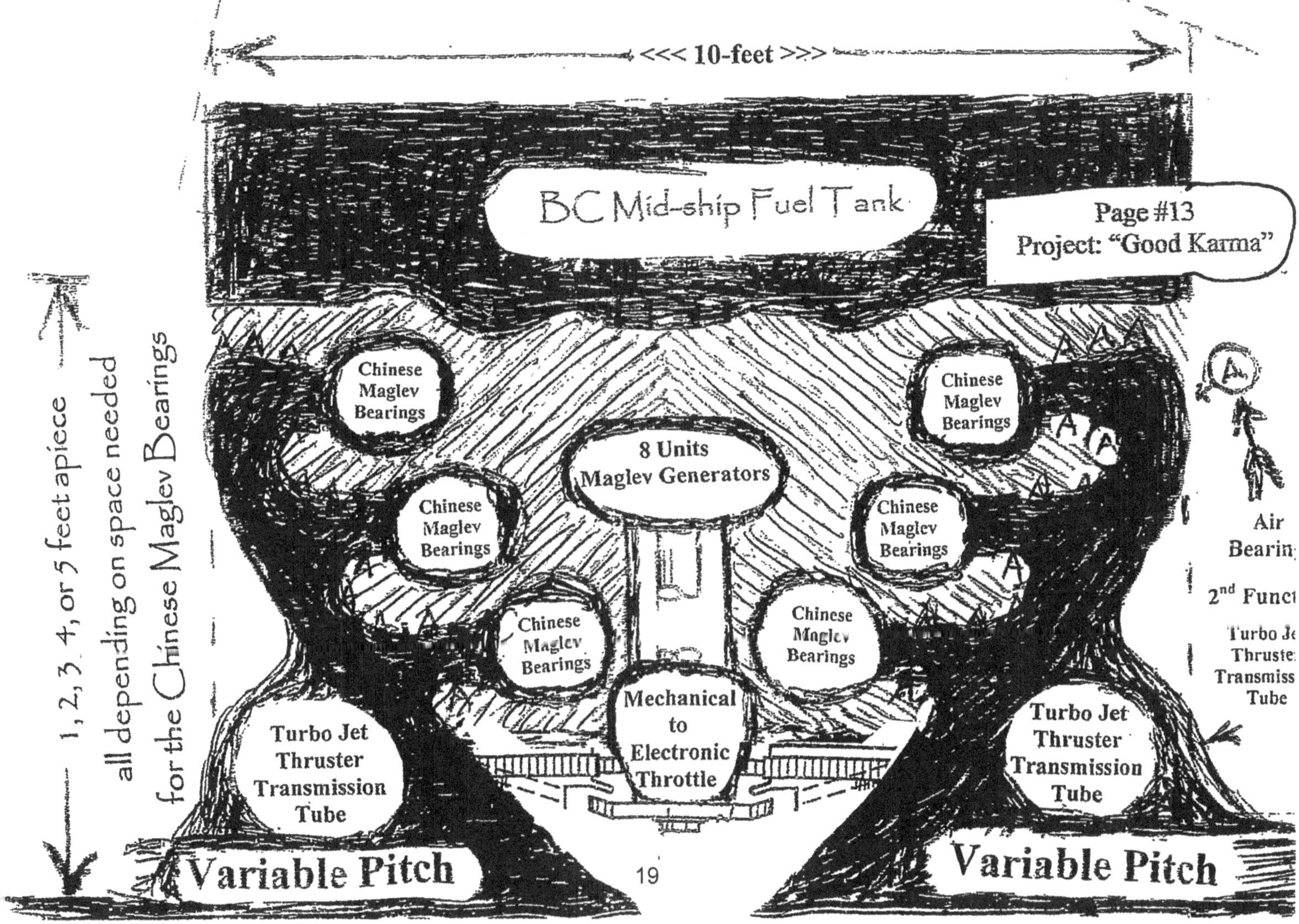

To the right is the last page
of my April 6th Phase I presentation
for the Meeting of the Presidents
Donald Trump and Xi Jinping.
All the Chinese characters
are drawn by hand.

Balance

With balance in our hearts, minds, souls, and nations the here-in Project: "Good Karma" begins.

Briefing Phase II:

Logically, I seek Pentagon interested people as the money required to develop this still unproven flight technology; Project: "Good Karma", will go to both NASA and our United States Armed Forces as we step forwards.

My first background letter document is dated:
November 07, 1973

7 November 1973

Mr. Steven N. DeSoto
105 West Mitchell
Milwaukee, Wisconsin 53204

Dear Mr. DeSoto:

Thank you for your recent letter.

At the present time we are doing little hiring. However, if you will complete and return one Personal Resume, we will review your qualifications in light of our openings and advise you further.

Your interest in the Agency is appreciated.

Sincerely,

D. H. Luetscher
Deputy Director of Personnel
for Recruitment and Placement

Enclosures

Page #17
Project: "Good Karma"

Dedicated to my brother

Captain Kirwin Shedd Webster

Capt. K. Shedd Webster, USN; during the Viet Nam War.
NROTC 1962-67, Commissioned 1967, Retired 1993.
Flew A-4 and A-7 aircraft primarily. 3000 + Hours,
600 + carrier landings and 100 + combat missions.

My brother Shedd is alive and well with his wife Pam in Colorado.
Shedd now works for a Ski Resort and lives for his kids and grandkids.

Page #18
Project: Good Karma"

Project: "Good Karma" R&D

#1: Testing the basic flight principal of compounding opposing wing-blades for VTO is simple enough. Use an air hose to gain RPMs desired on a horizontal contact location. No need to advance into the electric throttle or laser based throttle of our future years. Keep it simple with roller bearing or ball-bearings at first. I am not the science guy. I have just always wanted to build one of these aircraft designed after our own Milky Way.

The Test: The two wing-blades in opposition should out fly the two wing-blades in tandem; each with equal RPMs. Simply test with scales of a constant torque at a certain RPM.

#2: Parts: The most difficult part to develop is the Drive Beam. The Drive Beam is the RPM rail for the wing-blades. Those Drive Beams have multiple bearing assemblies; air, metal, maglev. Those Drive Beams support the total aircraft weight divisible only by the pairs of wing-blades we employ. Certainly the 9-Planet overview offers 8 sets of wing-blades with 8 sets of magnetic bearing housings within the engine-room areas. With positive computer flight probability analysis tests we can move forward seeking all nations to invest both time and money.

Fig. 5-A-9 is a Mother ship without a star wars theme. This Fig. 5-A-9
is an earth bound Aircraft designed after our very own Milky Way
Universe. Again the most difficult concept to put together is or are the
Drive Beams that ride within the maglev bearings. They must carry
enough copper to transmit/transfer electricity. They must also be
magnetic to balance within the maglev bearings; iron or a lighter element to
be designed that is still strong enough to lift the aircraft into flight.

I first thought of a yardstick made of a light iron ¼" x 1" x 36" twisted
once by 360-degrees and then reconnected end to end. Then we fill the
empty or void with copper. Then I thought of twisting that same drive
beam several times by 360-degrees then reconnecting. Once done we
round the circular/outer face with a strong sheet of contact alloy facing
the metal bearings. Next "R&D" is designing a balanced number of outer
casing pockets into which weapon grade lasers can be used as
propulsion/fuel to reach 30,000 plus RPMs. Instead of the yardstick
start with a processed 5 point star drive beam that is also twisted 360
degrees, once, or several times, and reattach. Again fill voids with copper
and finish the drive beam unit with a strong magnetic outer face. Then
design like pockets into which weapon grade lasers can be used for
advanced earth bound propulsion.

Overcome "Eternal War"
with a work of technological art designed after
our very own Milky Way Universe.

Patent Up-Date Continuance Pending Participation
Official USA Corporate/Government
Request Drafted: March 05, 2017

FIG. 5 -A - 9

This is the 9-Planet Overview

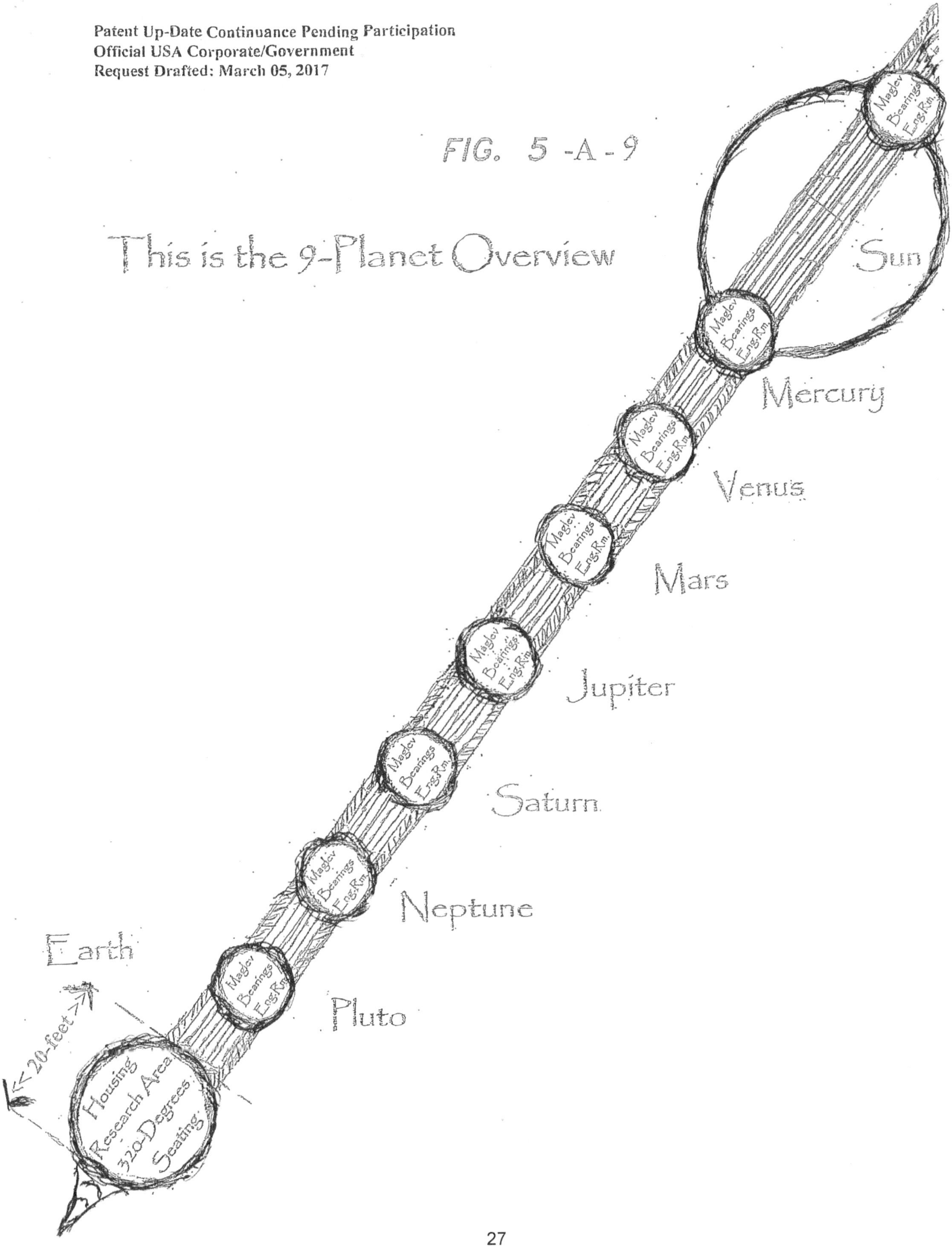

Senator Bill Nelson
413 Clematis Street, Suit #210
West Palm Beach, Florida 33401
Ph: 561-514-0189
Fax: 561-514-4078

April 03, 2017
Steven Nichols Webster
800 Uno Lago Drive, #203
Juno Beach, Florida 33406
Ph: 970-946-3858
DOB: 8/6/1946, Boston

Reference: USA/Chinese Technology Sharing.
Project: "Good Karma", Tricentric Aircraft VAu 48-797.
Do share Project: "Good Karma" with President Donald Trump
before Chinese President Xi Jinping arrives here in West Palm Beach.

Dear Senator Bill Nelson,

Sir, I thank you for your life of successful NASA missions and political representation here at home. I offer this Project: "Good Karma" towards China/USA relations while seeking Russia/NATO/Etc. participation. Please help me bring this Project: "Good Karma"; mechanical to electrical flight off the ground while Chinese President Xi Jinping comes to West Palm Beach to visit with President Donald Trump at Mar-a-Lago. Please represent me; a constituent. Our USA/CHINA relations need constant care. This is more than just one more project. You know my interest in NASA's Cassini May 2nd & 3rd, 2013 observations of a time I pray that never encompasses Earth with the same outcome. Please table Project: "Good Karma" with President Donald Trump before President Xi Jinping arrives.

Respectfully yours in Christ @ Sea & @ Home.
With Peace of Mind.

Nick Webster

Page #22
Project: "Good Karma"

Fax To: **202-636-0711**   April 06, 2017

FedEx Washington, D.C. Management   Nick Webster

snwebster@att.net

Ladies and Gentlemen,   970-946-3858

Long story short, Senator Bill Nelson sent Project: "Good Karma" to NASA not to the President Xi Jinping and President Trump meeting. Therefore, my earlier request to you folks to resend my PACKAGE Tracking # 786148945377 to the Chinese Embassy in D.C. would be up-staging Senator Nelson's NASA decision. I do NOT want to up-stage Senator Bill Nelson. Please, do not resend #786148945377 to the Washington D.C. Chinese Embassy. Thank you.

I will pay the difference tonight here in Juno Beach to re-lable that package in your D.C. facility to the following address:

Mr. Jared and Mrs. Ivanka Kushner
"American Innovation"
The White House
1600 Pennsylvania Ave. N.W.
Washington, D.C. 20500

They will understand and I will thus follow Senator Nelson's lead. The Chinese would prefer they receive their invitation to Project: "Good Karma" in Chinese. That would take me years.

Respectfully yours in Christ @ Sea & @ Home.
With Peace of Mind.

Nick Webster

26 Feb 2009

From: CAPT Dwight C. Fulton, Force Surgeon, Military Sealift Command

Subject: PHYSICAL QUALIFICATION STATUS ON STEVEN N. WEBSTER

1. Issues of Concern in reviewing Mr. Webster's medical information:

    a. Common Variable Lymphogammaglobulinemia. *COMSCINST 6000.1D - Any chronic condition which effects functional performance, is progressive, or, in the physician's opinion, may be worsened by the mariner's employment is considered disqualifying. Any condition, which poses a threat to the health and safety of the mariner, his/her shipmates or the ship, is considered disqualifying.* Date of diagnosis was 24 May 2004. Based on my review of the medical records submitted, Mr. Webster is followed by Oncology and Hematology for this diagnosis and his diagnosis of Non-Hodgkin's Lymphoma. For this diagnosis, he is currently on weekly subcutaneous dosing of gammaglobulin which he has been self-administering since at least October 2008. However, there is nothing in the records to indicate how he tolerates the treatments and if there have been any side effects related to the treatments. It was stated that his prognosis is good and that his risk of infection is low on the subcutaneous human gammaglobulin – i.e., same as normal individuals. However, as relates to contract operated MSC ships, I do have concerns about Mr. Webster's requirement for this ongoing parenteral therapy in a medical environment with a lack of medical expertise to manage any possible ramifications of the treatment. And, I have concerns about the possible clinical implications to the mariner of any interruption in his treatments due to unforeseen problems to his medical supplies or delivery systems. This may result in adverse consequences for both the health and safety of the mariner and for the mission of the ship if the ship has to divert in order to medically evacuate the mariner so that he can continue his treatments. Therefore, a waiver to work on MSC ships is not recommended for his diagnosis of Common Variable Lymphogammaglobulinemia requiring weekly parenteral dosing of human gammaglobulin. I would be glad to reconsider this recommendation if further information addressing my concerns regarding the human gammaglobulin is addressed.

    b. Non-Hodgkin's Lymphoma. *NAVMED P-117 – Current or history of malignant tumors is disqualifying. COMSCINST 6000.1D – Malignancy is not disqualifying in and of itself. Duty status will be determined by frequency of required follow-ups, tolerance of prescribed medications, and documentation of continued stability from personal physician.* Date of diagnosis – 04 June 2004. There is no record of reoccurrence but the records included for review do indicate that he was treated with Rituxan in November of 2007 that would indicate possible reoccurrence at that time requiring this specialized treatment. In a handwritten note from the Oncology and Hematology clinician dated 13 December 2008, it is stated that his low grade lymphoma is controlled currently on no treatment and that he is totally functional and able to perform his usual tasks of occupation. His prognosis is determined by his physician as excellent. Based on the fact that there is no indication that his cancer has progressed in the last year off of treatment, history of Non-Hodgkin's Lymphoma is disqualifying but a waiver for his diagnosis is approved. However, any reoccurrence of the lymphoma would require that a clinical package be resubmitted to MSC for reevaluation of his waiver for Non-Hodgkin's Lymphoma.

c. Squamous Cell Carcinoma. *NAVMED P-117 – Current or history of malignant tumors is disqualifying. COMSCINST 6000.1D – Malignancy is not disqualifying in and of itself. Duty status will be determined by frequency of required follow-ups, tolerance of prescribed medications, and documentation of continued stability from personal physician.* Mr. Webster underwent several procedures for squamous cell carcinoma located on the right anterior shoulder (first diagnosed on 28 October 2004 and last treated 16 January 2007). He also had a well differentiated squamous cell carcinoma of the left back excised in September 2007. His last recorded visit with dermatology was 15 February 2008 at which time he had multiple actinic keratoses of the upper back and arms treated with liquid nitrogen. He has received education on the use of SPF 15, sun avoidance, protective clothing, and monthly self-examination as preventive measures to the occurrence of new lesions. Based on the fact that he has no reported lesions presently, that he appears to be very attentive to the recurrence of new lesions, and that he is educated on measures that will help to prevent new lesions, history of squamous cell carcinoma is disqualifying but a waiver for his diagnosis is approved. Any reoccurrence of the squamous cell carcinoma would require that a clinical package be resubmitted for reevaluation of his waiver.

2. This mariner is not physically qualified for mariner duty on board MSC ships due to his history of Common Variable Lymphogammaglobulinemia, Non-Hodgkin's Lymphoma, and Squamous Cell Carcinoma. I recommend that he be waivered for his diagnoses of Squamous Cell Carcinoma and Non-Hodgkin's Lymphoma but NOT for the diagnosis of Common Variable Lymphogammaglobulinemia due to concerns related to his weekly requirement for parenteral administration of human gammaglobulin.

3. Thank you for the opportunity to review this mariner's medical package.

Respectfully,

Dwight C. Fulton

NASA Headquarters
Suite 5R30
Washington, D.C.
20546
Fax: 202-358-4338

March 7th, 2015
S. N. Webster
351 Zenith Lane
Juno Beach, Fl. 33408
561-635-2847

Dear NASA,

Kind Sirs, I have over extended myself in an observation of my own before checking with you of NASA to verify the observation is NASA verified. I used my interpretation of a May 2nd and May 3rd, 2013, Cassini, filming of the super storm on the North Pole of Saturn. My observations were before the hexagram observation that seems to be the apple of the moment over the internet. Allotropic configuration of minerals displaced by the storm I presume. Therein, I have not been able to relocate the filming in question that I did observe via the internet at least 10 times over the years.

Now, I am responsible for my words. I am responsible because I wrote about this observation as background material in an ally building document I sent to Speaker of the House John Boehner just last week. A hard copy will be arriving by mail; as per any internal request for verification.

Therein, I said this: "We need a ***Common Denominator*** in our dialogue with Russia. **Money is a good common denominator.** Our USA Industrial Complex has matured into space travel trajectory and accomplishments beyond expectation. Just for this moment keep your thoughts "Out of this world". Look at the May 2nd and May 3rd, 2013 NASA Cassini coverage of the super-storm on the North Pole of the planet Saturn., That hurricane spun or now spins in two directions at once. Truly, it is out of this world.
That combined counter-clockwise storm coupled with a clockwise storm of equal center maximum force seemed to gather enough force to reconstruct every molecule of what was once on solid ground. Perhaps water as we know it today had been on planet Saturn some 20 times longer than water has been here on earth and perhaps people there never learned to get along. This is my closing though on mending bridges between Russia, the USA, and the Middle East overcoming Eternal War."

#1: Before the observation of the magnetic hexagram or hexagram discussion of Cassini May 2nd and May 3rd, 2013 was there NASA

recognition of a super-storm on the North Pole of planet Saturn that did earnestly spin in two opposite directions at the same Time.
{{{{ Yes or No }}}}

#2: I never mentioned this #2 issue as I did wonder if NASA under first review did observe red the same. My observations went ever farther in seeing that same "Out of this world" super-storm. I actually saw an energy source above the storm that looked like a living donut made of winds and light that spun from the outside to the inside around and around at a speed that was incredibly beyond, seemingly wind approaching the speed of light. It hovered above the storm like a jelly fish only compact yet transparent and wobbling within the tandem motion between it and the super-storm. The donut shaped energy was much smaller than the storm. The energy wobbled as the spinning occurred around the shorter diameter of the donut moving in an up the outside and down the inside. The winds moved from the outside to the inside around the intercept rather than around the donut 360 shape. The 360 shape would be as it laid on a table, so to speak.

I know you have seen God in action as you have observed time as you have. I am honored to live in a time as NASA has honored we the population of earth with such incredible achievements as transferring observations from so far away. Evolution has occurred.

Change of Subject: Many good friends have asked me: "Where is the money going to come from?" I am speaking of money to employ beyond the standards of the Gold Standard. NASA, you are showing the world where the money is going to come from. I was writing Mr. Speaker John Boehner about that money to employ a growing world as we overcome Eternal War.

Respectfully yours in Christ @ Sea & @ Home.

With Peace of Mind.

____
Steven Nichols Webster

DEPARTMENT OF THE NAVY

NAVAL AIR SYSTEMS COMMAND
NAVAL AIR SYSTEMS COMMAND HEADQUARTERS
WASHINGTON, DC 20361

IN REPLY REFER TO

4200
AIR-303F

APR 29 1985

Steven Nichols Webster
351 Zenith Lane
Juno Beach, Florida 33408

Gentlemen:

The Naval Air Systems Command has received your proposal entitled, "Counter Atomic Attack System: One," dated 15 April 1985 and it has been routed to the cognizant office for review and assessment. Your interest in Naval Aviation is greatly appreciated. It is the policy of this Command to encourage the submission of new ideas in the form of unsolicited proposals which offer significant scientific or technological promise and to protect the proposals from unauthorized disclosure of the ideas they contain.

It is expected that the review and assessment will be completed within forty five working days. We will be in communication with you as soon as possible with the Command's response.

For any further information or questions, your Naval Air Systems Command contact point is Ms. Abby Dunlap, AIR-303F, (202) 692-7393 or 692-3376.

Sincerely,

J.J. MULQUIN
Director, Technology Transfer Division
Research and Technology Group
By direction of the Commander
Naval Air Systems Command

Page #28
Project: "Good Karma"

DEPARTMENT OF THE AIR FORCE

WRIGHT LABORATORY (AFMC)
WRIGHT-PATTERSON AIR FORCE BASE, OHIO

1 6 MAY 1997

Recieved July 23

WL/FI-3 Building 45
2130 Eighth Street Suite 1
Wright-Patterson AFB OH 45433-7542

Mr. Nick Webster
12 Country Club Drive E
Destin FL 35241

Dear Mr. Webster

Thank you for your interest in sharing your air vehicle design concept with the US Air Force. AFMC Headquarters initially received your package and forwarded it to the Flight Dynamics Directorate of Wright Laboratory for consideration.

Unfortunately, the level of resources that would be required to fully analyze your concept are not currently available for such a high risk investment. First, Wright Laboratory is focusing all it's energy solely on fixed-wing aircraft, whereas the Army's focus is solely on rotary wing aerodynamic vehicles. Secondly, reduced budgets and reduced work force within the laboratory require that any unsolicited vehicle design concept must include a thorough and complete analysis to fully quantify how the vehicle offers a state-of-the-art improvement beyond the current fleet. Such an analysis is required for the full range of vehicle qualities such as agility, maneuverability, survivability, cost, range, etc.

If you choose to approach the Army, or any other US Government organization with your concept, I recommend that you utilize the information available on the internet to ensure the organization is specifically interested in the type of technology you are offering, and to create a marketable format which clearly defines the technological leap that your design offers. You might find it useful to review Air Force guidance on submitting an unsolicited proposal, which is posted at:

http://www.afmc.wpafb.af.mil/organizations/HQ-AFMC/PK/pkt/unsolpro.htm.

I wish you success in the continued development of your concept, and I hope your continued participation at refereed technical conferences will help you to build the resume and meet the professional contacts you will need to attract funding.

Sincerely

MARK S. MAURICE
Assistant Chief Scientist
Flight Dynamics Directorate

Enc:
Proposal Folder

Page # 29
Project: "Good Karma"

IN REPLY REFER TO

4200
Ser: AIR 2.1.1/016-17
10 Aug 2017

Mr. Steven N. Webster
Project "Good Karma"
PO Box 1
Atlantic Beach, NC 28512

Dear Mr. Webster,

The purpose of this letter is to return the enclosed unsolicited proposal, Project "Good Karma". The Federal Acquisition Regulations are very specific as to the requirements for an unsolicited proposal to be considered valid. As noted in FAR 15.603(c), an unsolicited proposal must: (1) be innovative and unique; (2) be independently originated and developed by the offeror; (3) be prepared without Government supervision, endorsement, direction, or direct Government involvement; (4) include sufficient detail to permit a determination that Government support could be worthwhile and the proposed work could benefit the agency's research and development or other mission responsibilities; (5) not be an advance proposal for a known agency requirement that can be acquired by competitive methods, and (6) not address a previously published agency requirement.

The proposal, as submitted, is innovative and unique; however it does not support our agency's research and development efforts and other mission responsibilities. Additionally, NAVAIR does not currently have the resources required to fully analyze your concept.

Although your submission can not be accepted for consideration as an unsolicited proposal at NAVAIR, your interest in supporting the needs of this command and the U.S. Navy is appreciated. I would recommend that you review SUB-Net and FEDBIZOPPS regularly for other opportunities to do business with the U.S. Government. The web sites are http://web.sba.gov/subnet/ and www.fbo.gov respectively.

If you have any questions, please contact Tonecia Porter at 301-757-2536 or at tonecia.porter@navy.mil.

Respectfully,

Dana C. Veitch
Division Head
Contract Policy and Process Management Division

Enclosure: Project "Good Karma" Proposal

President Donald J. Trump
The White House
1600 Pennsylvania Ave. NW
Washington, DC 20500
202-456 1414
202-208-1631

Memorial Day Weekend
May 26th, 2018

S. N. Webster
400 Money Island Drive
Atlantic Beach, North Carolina 28512
nickwebster1946@outlook.com
970-846-3858

Reference: Enclosed 88 page booklet on Project: "Good Karma".

First Requested Issue: United States Armed Forces enlistment options to include developing and protecting our United States Armed Forces ongoing "R&D" on Project: "Good Karma" in coordination with our present China assisted North Korean Nuclear Disarmament proceedings.

Statement by S. N. Webster: Our Armed Forces enlistment participation is expected to increase 10-fold with the inclusion of Project: "Good Karma".

To: The Honorable President of the United States of America
    President Donald John Trump,

Sir, this 2018 Memorial Day Weekend we honor those whom have given the ultimate sacrifice to keep America free. We honor the families of all those fallen servicemen and servicewoman. We honor the wounded. We honor all those still in uniform, we give our thanks and praise to all our Armed Forces.

Today we are working together as world partners keeping North Korea's Nuclear Disarmament in focus. Our United States Armed Forces must make the target threat validating militaristic technological advancement obvious. Incoming meteorites to be harvested are my first thoughts for your conversations on the subject with North Korea. I do want to work with you and for your team, our country, our USA. We Sir; you and I Sir, are the same age both being born in 1946. We are working on the same project under different names. I ask for your recognition and support of my request for NASA to accept developing "R&D" for Project: "Good Karma".

Yes, the private sector does also want to study, share, and invest just to assure there is an active "R&D" on the likes of Project: "Good Karma".

Yes, the separation of "Fake News" and the "Truth" will have its day as our USA, China, North Korea, EU, Russia, and world develop the technology needed to fly Project: "Good Karma". After all, it is your Trump Presidency that this Project: "Good Karma" is now timed within.

Our veterans are our representatives today, this Memorial Day Weekend. Our United States of America stands free today because our veterans freely stood bravely in harms way. We do remember and today again honor our fallen veterans. May we; The United States of America, stand freely to "Overcome Eternal War".

Respectfully yours in Christ @ Sea, @ Home, & in the Sky.

With PEACE of mind.

Nick Webster
Free Agent SNW – License Pending

United States Attorney General Jefferson B. Sessions   March 26, 2018
United States Department of Justice
950 Pennsylvania Avenue NW   Project: "Good Karma"
Washington, D.C. 20530-0001   Free Agent SNW - Unlicensed
                                              S. N. Webster
                                              400 Money Island Drive
                                              Atlantic Beach, N. C. 28512
                                              Contact: 970-946-3858

Reference: Project: "Good Karma"; centralizing the proposed computer
based Flight Probability Analysis with NASA while seeking financial
support from private, public/corporate, and international interests.

   I; S.N. Webster, here-in request President Donald Trump to approve
   this Project: "Good Karma" as unproven and to be developed with-in
   traditional financial, technological, and aviation standards recorded
   within NASA as a civilian request.

The Honorable Attorney General Jefferson B. Sessions,

Sir, there is Peace in my heart and Peace in my objective of seeking
President Donald Trump's approval of this Project: "Good Karma". I have
attached my letter to Elon Musk seeking Spacex participation. Having a
public USA Team effort in developing this aircraft/spacecraft is essential to
our Peace Process Agenda as a country.

The timelessness of this project rests gently with our first manned Apollo
Moon Landing and NASA's announced study within the unknown physics
of Warp Speed via a Quantum Vacuum Thruster. A Project: "Good Karma"
"R&D" study within earth's atmosphere is here and now referred as a
micro/macro equivalence to NASA's desired/developing Warp Speed
Studies substituting intergalactic distance with earth bound fuel
regeneration. The logic of carrying this circular flight objective within
NASA; a flying generator sustaining non-nuclear fuel regeneration within
our atmosphere, out weighs the catchy phrase; "Designed after our very own
spiral universe the Milky Way".

Respectfully yours in Christ @ Sea & @ Home.

With Peace of Mind.

Nick Webster

April 4ᵗʰ, 2018

Briefing: Recent Public {1-on-1} Discussion, Project: "Good Karma"

Two very respectable friends of mine brought out two very direct and seemingly popular opinions while discussing the logic of my success in my international effort to build an aircraft/spacecraft designed in the likeness of our very own spiral galaxy the Milky Way. Why symbolize our nation's efforts in "Overcoming Eternal War" technologically? We will discuss funding concepts after these other two points of view have been established as #1 and #2. In truth, funding builds the aircraft/spacecraft.

#1: 2018; Questioning the probability of "Overcoming Eternal War".
#1: <> "There are simply too many people on Earth. The population of Earth doubled just a few decades ago." My rebuttal: "I do want to employ those generations to come; those now considered an oncoming over-population problem. It will take more than the Gold System was designed for to employ such a maturing population.

#2: 2018; Questioning the logic of "Overcoming Eternal War".
#2: <> Christ said: "There will always be wars and rumors of wars."
My rebuttal: "I am a Christian by choice and by life experience. Christ also spoke of the End of the Age and said "You will always hear about wars and rumors about wars... Be not alarmed." Every language known to mankind be it written in stone, or on papyrus, or parchment, paper, or on i-phones was and now is written in the waning of the Ice Age. On the North Pole this February and March of 2018 were the first temperatures above freezing ever recorded. I know this is a change of subject. Mindfully, it will take a lot more money rebuilding both the private and public sectors than the Gold System had planned for if Mother Nature rains, snows, and blows all our polar zones back our way.

I prefer to pray for a gentle transition to frozen equatorial atmospheric rings like our neighbor planet Saturn.

<u>A prayer in closing:</u>

Christ; I pray you will enjoy and bless our efforts to love humanity as we attempt to "Overcome Eternal War" in thought, word, and deed technologically through the End of this Ice Age and unto our next atmospheric continuance.

Respectfully yours in Christ @ Sea, in the sky, & @ Home,
With Peace of Mind,

Nick Webster
Nick Webster

Chairman Senator Richard Burr
U. S. Senate Select Committee on Intelligence
211 Hart Senate Office Building
Washington, D. C.   20510
202-224-1700

March 4th, 2018

Steven Nichols Webster
400 Money Island Drive
Atlantic Beach, N. C. 28512
970-946-3858

Reference: Project: "Good Karma" requests your support Senator Burr. North Carolina is and always will be the "First in Flight". Please help me get this mission to manifest off the ground in North Carolina style; in the public eye.

The Honorable Senator Richard Burr,

Sir, I was schooled by the Outer Banks' very own Captain Jim Zook of Morehead City in 1984. That same November I tested and received my first USCG Captain's License. My medical discharge from the Military Sealift Command in 2009 is included in the attached Project: "Good Karma". I am Nick Webster, I ask for your support Sir. Many truths are self evident. This time sensitive international objective of "Overcoming Eternal War" is a reality. President Donald Trump has yet to comment on my project.

Change of subject: Did you hear that this March 2018 marked another first; the first temperatures above freezing were recorded on our North Pole. In this waning of this Ice Age civilization has produced all written languages known today; be they written in stone, or clay, or on papyrus, and paper, even now on smart phones. Sir, I want my Project: "Good Karma" to become a household conversation. China and Russia would love to take part in this project. Switzerland has been working to produce "anti-mater' for almost a decade. Their dreams becoming reality would make my dreams all the easier to get off the ground. In that light I can only hope our USA Team in Area 51 has flown an adaptation of my tricentric U.S. Patent # 5,213-284 as per my U.S. Design Patent #320-378; as having already built an aircraft/spacecraft designed after our very own spiral galaxy the Milky Way.

Respectfully yours in Christ @ Sea & @ Home.

With Peace of mind,

Nick Webster

Congressman Richard Burr / SNW   03/04/2018

In Closing:

God bless America !

We the citizens of these United States of America are blessed with
certain inalienable rights; such as the pursuit of happiness. Over the
years this flight project has brought me much happiness. The project
name has changed from Counter Atomic Attack System One;
Operation: Cultivation of the Stars while concentrating on USA-
USSR nuclear disarmament in the 80's and 90's into today's Project:
"Good Karma" while now concentrating on USA-China/North
Korean nuclear disarmament.

I do hope and pray that these humble pages reflect respect and represent
our nation's values as viewed from both our Red and our Blue
democratically elected House of Representatives and our United
States Senate.

In God we trust.

Steven Nichols Webster

Elon Musk
Spacex
1030 15th Street N.W.
Suite 220E
Washington, D.C. 20005-1503
310-363-6000

February 23, 2018
Nick Webster
400 Money Island Drive
Atlantic Beach, N.C. 28512
970-946-3858

Reference: Mission to manifest request for Project: "Good Karma".

Mr. Elon Musk, Sir.

In brief; I ask you to consider my enclosed Project: "Good Karma" worthy of completion. You Sir could complete my lifetime dream within these pages. Therein you must decide. I ask you to enter a bid request for NASA approval for a computer based Flight Probability Analysis of Project: "Good Karma". You know the business needs that Tesla, Spacex, and Boring have manifested to accomplish technological advancements like my offering needs. I need an industrial leader like you to see my dream come true.

I turned 71 years young this past summer; 08/06/1946. An 8-hour work day is now beyond my grasp. Enough said; I am not asking you to employ me as much as champion the task of adding NASA based interest in completing Project: "Good Karma". My dreams are not in taking; flying, this aircraft to other planets. This is an Earth-bound spacecraft/aircraft and not intended to be our next traditional interplanetary spacecraft. At this point I am simply setting limits to the expectations I feel you will enjoy completing, Sir.

Your computer banks on metallurgy, tribology, and electronics should be perfectly capable of producing a functional tricentric aircraft and thereafter a 9-planet plan spacecraft/aircraft as described within.

Respectfully yours in Christ @ Sea & @ Home.

With PEACE of mind.

Nick Webster

February 23, 2018

To: Elon Musk and the Spacex, Tesla, Boring Team

The following was prepared as an unsolicited presentation to last years
Meeting of President Trump and President Jinping, on April 06, 2017.

I have found the political reasons forgoing the development of
international/technology/sharing as stated or requested in my original
presentation to be two-sided. That discussion will prayerfully be held in
our United States Senate and our United States House of
Representatives soon.

My present objective is to secure a USA Team capable of a
successful "R&D", nut and bolt, VTO, computed test run prior to that
congressional conversation/debate.

Thank you for your time and consideration.

Nick Webster

In Closing:

Mr. Elon Musk and envisioned Spacex, Tesla, Boring Team,

As you well know by now I am not an architect. I am not even a
science guy. Yet as the Good Lord Christ knows, I can dream.

I do hope that you do fly with success, drive with success, and
bore with success. I do hope you make many more dreams a
success. I do hope to work with you on this project reality.

Respectfully yours in Christ @ Sea & @ Home

Mr. Nick Webster

Congresswoman Nancy Pelosi   February 25th, 2018
233 Cannon House Office Building   Steven Nichols Webster
Washington, D. C. 20515   400 Money Island Dr.
202-225-4966   Atlantic Beach, N.C. 28512
                                              970-946-3858

Reference: Congressional recognition and if necessary debate
            supporting Project: "Good Karma".
Herein presented by S. N. Webster, DOB: 08/06/1946, Boston.

The Honorable Congresswoman Nance Pelosi,

Our country stands divided on money issues to an extent unknown since
the mid 1800's. Only the sorrow shared losing 17 souls; students, shot in
Broward County this month holds a universal feeling our country shares
equally from both the blue and the red. Therein join me in a moment of
silence and PEACE as we work and pray to see school shootings stop.
Amen!

While real Peace in our nation's schools is a congressional issue in
debate; I support an 18 or older age limit for the purchasing of firearms.
In that same breath bump-stocks should be classified within the same
category as fully automatic firearms.

In the bigger picture of international Peace and our United States of
America's effort to "Overcome Eternal War" I present the enclosed
flight program; Project: "Good Karma", as an internationally funded
project. That "internationally funded" with "technology sharing" specific
to that aircraft/spacecraft vs. a "private" funding agenda may or may not
need/reach congressional debate. Mr. Elon Musk and his Tesla,

Spacex, and Boring Team will receive an invitation this week to seek a mission to manifest NASA bid for that computer based Flight Probability Analysis outcome. Yes, I feel Mr. Elon Musk could develop the needed "USA Team" computer generated Flight Probability Analysis I requested via Senator Bill Nelson's West Palm Beach Office when on April 6th, 2017 Senator Nelson sent my Project: "Good Karma" to NASA.

Congresswoman Nancy Pelosi, I am not a well educated flight engineer. I have never had a "face to face encounter of the 3rd kind". From the hearts and minds of citizens of many countries; both well educated and preschoolers, will come the successful development of the aircraft/spacecraft designed after our very own spiral galaxy;

The Milky Way.

These are big words, big dreams, big plans, and will find the financial support needed. I ask you Congresswoman Nancy Pelosi, I ask you to seek a deserving round of applause as you carry Project: "Good Karma" before our United States Congress.

Respectfully yours in Christ @ Sea & @ Home.

With PEACE of mind.

Nick Webster

To:
Mayor A. B. "Trace" Cooper
Town of Atlantic Beach
125 West Fort Macon Road
Atlantic Beach, N. C. 28512
252-723-2066

Wednesday September 27, 2017
Free Agent SNW
Steven Nichols Webster
400 Money Island Drive
Atlantic Beach, N. C. 28512
970-946-3858

Reference: North Carolina First In Flight.

Dear Mayor Cooper,

Back in the 1980's and 1990's I introduced the enclosed as the mission aircraft in a USA/USSR Nuclear Disarmament Program entitled Counter Atomic Attack, System One: Operation: Cultivation of the Stars. Communism collapsed and the international space station took center stage.

In 1984 Capt. Zook of Salter Path trained a handful of local fishermen in preparation for our USCG Captain's License testing. I was one of those fortunate seamen. I left the fishing industry for the oil and gas industry. I retested and advanced my officer status every five years thanks to Capt. Zook, Capt. Harlan Murphy of Beaufort, Capt. George Huthmatcher of Charleston, and many other memorable and honorable captains.

As the title of this presentation leads we are now reviewing aviation from our inspired beginnings to beyond today's flight ready fleet. I intend to help inspire North Carolinians to dare to go beyond as our Star Wars counterpart has enacted before. We will build this aircraft or one better with N. C. and D. C. interested in the education there-of as suggested here-in. Perhaps you would enjoy the last pages of this presentation first.

In closing:

Mr. Mayor Trace Cooper, I would be honored if you would verify my
story via your office phone by calling Senator Bill Nelson's West Palm
Beach Office or Washington, D. C. Office. I expect an extended
NASA computer based Flight Probability Analysis.

Senator Bill Nelson
Hart Senate Office Building
Washington, D.C. 20002
202-228-2183

Senator Bill Nelson
413 Clematis Street, Suit 210
West Palm Beach, Florida
561-514-4078

Mr. Mayor Sir, China has joined our United States of America with
our sanctioning North Korea into an end to North Korea's
"War Dance". One step at a time is all we can work towards. We are
many individuals moving in many directions as is our normal everyday
agenda by town, county, state, country.

Respectfully yours in Christ @ Sea & @ Home.
With Peace of Mind.

Nick Webster
Nick Webster
Free Agent SNW

Ambassador Nikki R. Haley
U. S. Mission to the United Nations
U. S. Department of State
2201 C Street N.W.
Washington, DC 20318-0000

July 21, 2017
Nick Webster
Free Agent, unlicensed
C/o
POB #1, Mr. Walter Curry
Atlantic Beach, N.C. 28512
970-946-3858

Reference: Unsolicited "R&D" Proposal, Project: "Good Karma"

Cover Letter 2-Pages

Sir Ambassador Nikki R. Haley,

An honor Sir! I do expect an extended NASA computer based Flight Probability Analysis. NASA's experts only have to analyze flight probability for Earth bound flights under Project: "Good Karma". My main concern is at your level, that you hear no fake news first. Not to have any "Fake News" on my Project: "Good Karma" is nearly impossible. Funding is the one thing I have overlooked since the early 90's till today.

Sir, the physics supporting the logic of design in tricentric displacement is far easier to test as a watercraft. The structural physics; as per a watercraft, are well known today. Water could be moved by wing-blades from both top and bottom, then compressed, and channeled to compliment a forward intake to an aft ship thruster. Such a watercraft would steer by fins, compressing water into jets, and of-course a rudder if need be; say an intake area became clogged with fish bones, etc.

The physics supporting the aircraft could certainly redirect air to assist in steering to supplement wing flaps with direct blasts of air at slow speeds and while hovering. Today we have NASA as our Peace Time application of national technological resources. Project: "Good Karma" simply gives our world's top 10 Super Powers a group technological project to work on together independently and/or jointly. When nations disagree as to the best solution to any given technological issue within the Project: "Good Karma" mission aircraft they will be encouraged to advance their hypothesis independently or jointly and announce the superior finding when found. International participation should lower cost of production per nation/state by 75%. However, not wanting to overcome the "Eternal War" issue by immerging or existing nation states would support the status quo of yesteryear's and today's defense strategies as most appropriate. We need the top 10 super powers to work on a project such as Project: "Good Karma".

In closing I offer three {3} statements to quell the possible "Fake News" claims sighting a "Face to Face Encounter of a Third Kind" being the reason for Project: "Good Karma". #1: I, S.N. Webster, the author of Project: "Good Karma" have never had a "face to face" encounter of the third kind; extra terrestrial encounter. #2: NASA has recently announced observing several suns and all their planets issuing like radio signals opening the possibility of civilization having reached and cultivated several sun based galaxies as of this date. #3: Finding/observing a "face to face" encounter with an advanced inter-galactic civilization having achieved "Peace" after or before we produce Project: "Good Karma" would be enjoyable.

Respectably yours in Christ @ Sea & @ Home.
With Peace of Mind.

____

S. N. Webster

General Joseph F. Dunford Jr.
Chairman of the Joint Chief of Staff
9999 Joint Staff Pentagon
Washington, DC 20318-0000

July 21, 2017
Nick Webster
Free Agent SNW - unlicensed
C/o
POB #1, Mr. Walter Curry
Atlantic Beach, N.C. 28512
970-946-3858

Reference: Unsolicited "R&D" Proposal, Project: "Good Karma"

Cover Letter 2-Pages

General Joseph F. Dunford Sir,

An honor Sir! I do seek your approval for Project: "Good Karma" funding. Funding is the one thing I have overlooked since the early 90's till today.

Sir, the physics supporting the logic of design in tricentric displacement is far easier to test as a watercraft. The structural physics; as per a watercraft, are well known today. Water could be moved by wing-blades from both top and bottom, then compressed, and channeled to compliment a forward intake to an aft ship thruster. Such a watercraft would steer in the water by compressing water into jets, fins, and of-course a rudder if need be; say an intake area or propulsion area became clogged with fish bones, etc.

The physics supporting the aircraft could certainly redirect air to assist in steering to supplement wing flaps with direct blasts of air at slow speeds and while hovering. Today we have NASA as our Peace Time application of national technological resources. Project: "Good Karma" simply gives our world's top 10 Super Powers a group technological project to work on together independently and/or jointly. When nations disagree as to the best solution to any given technological issue within the Project: "Good Karma" mission aircraft they will be encouraged to advance their hypothesis independently or jointly and announce their superior finding when found. International participation should lower cost of production per nation/state by 75%. However, not wanting to overcome the "Eternal War" issue by immerging or existing nation states would support the status quo of yesteryear's and today's defense strategies as most appropriate. We need at least the top 10 super powers to work on Project: "Good Karma".

In closing I offer three {3} statements to quell the possible "Fake News" claims sighting a "Face to Face Encounter of a Third Kind" being the reason for Project: "Good Karma".

#1: I; S.N. Webster, the author of Project: "Good Karma" have never had a "face to face" encounter of the third kind; extra terrestrial encounter.
#2: NASA has recently announced observing several suns and all their planets issuing like radio signals opening the possibility of civilization having reached and cultivated several sun based galaxies as of this date.
#3: Finding/observing a "face to face" encounter with an advanced inter-galactic civilization having achieved "Peace" after or before we produce Project: "Good Karma" would be enjoyable.

Respectably yours in Christ @ Sea & @ Home.
With Peace of Mind.

————————————

S. N. Webster

4ᵗʰ of July Brief

On the
Water Glass Policy

Presented to: ECOFIN Council
Economic and Financial Affairs
Council of the European Union
Rue de la Loi 175
B-1048 Brussels
Contact: {32-2} 281-61-11
Fax: {32-2} 281-69-34

Presented by: S.N. Webster
Free Agent SNW
351 Zenith Lane
Juno Beach, Florida 33408
Contact: 1-561-568-3265
 Fax: 1-561-626-6149

Objective:

The objective of this brief is to pay our United States National Debt in my life-time. I have Non-Hodgkin's' Lymphoma. 50% of us live 5-years. This is my 5ᵗʰ-year. I am Steven Nichols Webster, born in Boston on August 06, 1946. We citizens of these United States of America are divided as to how to pay our United States National Debt. The family is our basic unit. This we agree on. I believe in God. I accept Jesus Christ as my Lord, King, and Savior. We do not all feel the same in the USA. Our United States of America is host to many religions, tribes, races and opinions on many subjects. I will be sending this 4ᵗʰ of July 2010 Brief on the Water Glass Policy, to my Florida State and Federal Senators and Representatives, United States President Barack Obama, my Juno Beach Mayor Mort Levine, and my Juno Beach Council Members.

I request that the Economic and Financial Affairs ECOFIN Council of the European Union accept to review and consider developing the needed second phase of Alpha Economic Growth of the EURO and present same to the G-8. There-in all national treasuries could grow at a standard and basic Pi 3.14159 % for a predetermined duration of time for the public good.

The purpose of this 4th of July 2010 Brief
is to have the European Union accept the concept of our paying off our
United States National Debt with Alpha Currency,
Alpha and Omega Currency explained here-in on page #3.

$$\Pi \quad \pi$$

Pi is the 16th letter in the Greek Alphabet
Alpha is the first letter and Omega is the last letter

**Universally, π Pi is known as the ratio of a
circle's circumference to its diameter**

or

$$\pi = 3.14159$$

Pi Π ; the upper-case letter is used as a symbol for the **product operator**
in mathematics.

Pi Π ; the upper-case letter in legal shorthand to represent the **plaintiff**.

Pi π ; the lower-case letter is used as a symbol for **Profit**
in microeconomics.

Pi π ; the lower-case letter is also used as a symbol for **Inflation Rate**
in macroeconomics.

Pi π ; the lower-case letter is also used as a symbol for the
Prime counting function in mathematics.

*** All references to Pi were taken from Wikipedia the free on-line encyclopedia**

3.14159

π

Aα Ωω
Alpha Omega

FINANCIALLY

Alpha is the beginning the date of issue	Omega is the accomplishment of all time, as we look back
Alpha money is new money fresh off the mint press	Omega money is old money already used and owned
In this case Alpha Money would be issued to pay off our USA National Debt	The option will be to pay our USA National Debt out of our pockets out of our existing funds from our bank accounts as per individual means

From Revelation 22:13 KJV; The New Testament has God himself to be the "Alpha and Omega, the beginning and the end, the first and the last."

Here we visualize the two legs of Pi   π   as Alpha and Omega for the financial purpose of paying off our USA National Debt and ending eternal inflation, by employing the Pi 3.14159 factor as a national treasury growth standard for the industrialized world for a predetermined period of time. There-in the basic family household would be less burdened with taxation during that time period and the national/state/county objectives of health and education will be subsidized there-with. The cost of employing an elected government would remain tax-based. **However,** the USA cannot go this path alone lest we end up paying $1,000,000.oo USD for a 12-oz Coca-cola ourselves. It is time to bite the bullet. There-with the G-8, G20, and G-40 and finally the United Nations would need to assume a National Treasury Growth Standard for all stages of national growth; presumably the same 3.14159 %. Because lesser developed nation/states would gain less advantage than developed nation/states, additional financial support for the lesser developed nation/states will remain on the table for development.

SNW

4th of July 2010 Brief

As the Plaintiff in this argument before our United States of America and our great neighbors beyond I submit this **4th of July 2010 Brief** for opening this vote based government regulated United States National Debt payment option entitled the **Water Glass Policy.** Because our United States of America remains divided as to a national treasury expansion factor I am acting independently of political party seeking the Economic and Financial Affairs ECOFIN Council of the European Union to review this concept for discussion of balancing growth factors within the EURO by coordinating Growth Expansion Factors in the EURO with G-8 discussion of like-form there with-in. Austerity seeks past standards with a 25-year growth period yielding a recession with a history of war without common base factors eluding that reoccurring 25-year or so recession. The mirror image of the EURO unchanged would be the Republican Standard in the USA and a standard that has reached a matured strategy stage with a very satisfactory commodity marketplace exchange medium for most macro industries be they fast food chains, grocery stores, tool outlets, clothing lines and basic need items; all have success stories in the channeled financial markets and success with gratitude at the lower income levels as well. However, a universal demand for improving that Austerity Standard has been tabled world wide because the basic 3% inflation rate sponsored at every upper level within the Free Enterprise System has developed a financial market presence that out valued the substance management side sold to investors outside their microeconomic objective thus dividing the macroeconomic equation leaving the incoming microeconomic participants caught without the financial means. Because the USA is now politically divided as to an intellectual resolve of economic equation I present this the **"Water Glass Policy"**; so named because water takes the form of that which holds it. Water also seeks the lowest common denominator towards sea-level if not held. Today even sea-level is a constant concern because of our melting Polar Zones. This factor of seemingly unnatural formation novelty was not even written into standard educational text when I was born 63 years ago. Within our most recent decades we have translated the Mayan Calendar to represent the end of a cycle explained via observation of the planets and stars to predict this polar eclipse so-to-speak. This completion of the Mayan Calendar is predicted be about 12/10/2012. A beginning is also presumed self-evident after the date: 12/10/2012. We must wait and see. Again reviewing this proposed Water Glass Policy, one fills a water glass from the bottom to the top and the glass runneth other at the top where our tax systems of modern day democracies take hold. The date: 12/10/2012 represents a time of visibly heightened universal light caused through a universal alignment corresponding with gravitational and rotational competition to be cause enough to induce remarkable change among the normal elements of change we know as seasons, man-made structures, etc. With this date approaching and the challenges of technology gone wrong; as in the Deep Horizon BP Oil Spill in the Golf of Mexico, economic compromise within this same time-window when natural disasters may evolve faster than intellectual economic solutions would be foolish. Within the scenario of disasters; spending is a necessary element. Spending is the focus of the divide in the USA today. The particulars of this divide over spending reaches no permanent economic solution, only the realization that there is no macroeconomic equation covering all national democracies be they in their primal, standard, or matured industrial phase of development; be they primarily industrial, agricultural, ,tourist based, or in a family based tribal state of growth. Again there is no macroeconomic equation internationally. Independence is the common choice between a One World Economy and working with and by the standards of today. I also agree that a One World Economy would develop the provider farther above the common need and separate the management from the traditional population. Thus with this said and understood I; Steven Nichols Webster, act in a Free Agent capacity as Free Agent SNW do seek the assistance of my state and federal representatives, our United` States President Barack Obama, The Economic and financial Affairs Council of the European Union, the G-8, and basically the nations holding our USA Treasury Bonds and USA Treasury Notes to consider our USA payment there-of through Alpha Currency as explained in this 4th of July, 2010 Brief.

There are obstacles that stand before the Water Glass Policy that we can overcome with a unified objective.

Some years back I was fortunate enough to have shore leave in Turkey. There I had the novel experience of paying $1,000,000.oo paper Turkish currency for a 12 ounce Coca-Cola. I thought and thought about that million dollar soda and well. I do not want to deflate our USD. Nor do you want to deflate the EURO. Our cause is to avoid the growing separation between the haves and have-nots. Our cause is avoid a 25-year reoccurring recession. Our cause is to pay off our USA National Debt as soon as possible.

Again, I recall a time during your European Union formation. While I was 3rd Officer of the Christian Hospital Ship; the Caribbean Mercy, I wrote in favor of your EURO saying. "The EURO holds the credentials of inevitable success based on the preposition that the European Union is forming among nations/countries/states with a history of war against said same nations/countries/states; one against the other, hosting revolution, after revolution from the beginning of their written history to this day. Yet that same European Union's objective is to unite that war torn competitive history under an objective whence what-ever sector nation/country/state advances victorious there with-in all shall prosper, no sector nation/country/state will be left without, all shall gain as the other prospers."

We can make this Water Glass Policy work all around the world with independent treasuries and caring neighbors. By the European Union allowing our United States of America to pay off all of our national debt via new Alpha currency; same paper currency as yesterday, the G-8 would be next to review this option. In this acceptance the world can repair the wounds of the past as they themselves build from the lessons of the past and build a future for themselves under their own national currency and possibly rebuild that future in our lifetime in a well balanced manor and without abandoning their nation. I project with acceptance of the Water Glass Policy this earth will hold 10-times the representation in national currency in 300-years time, to do the same job better over and above today in 300-years time. That growth would be a National Treasury Growth rate of Pi or 3.14159% replacing 50% of household taxation rather than expanding government spending as the only priority objective. While the wealthiest of wealthy; whom purchased our United States National Treasury Bonds and United States National Treasury Notes must know the burden of payment must come. Fill the water glass from the bottom to the top, tax the overflow, enjoy your success. We will pay our USA National Debt out of our pockets or represent a Water Glass Policy formalizing a standardized basic national treasury growth equation of Pi 3.14159. Thank you for your time and consideration.

Respectfully yours in Christ @ Sea & @ Home.

Steven Nichols Webster
Free Agent SNW

Per-Capita Theory
"Out of this World"

Per-Capita Theory is a futuristic international economic growth and stability program enacted at the national level all around the civilized world.

This next question is a winner. <> How many times have you said: "Yes", that seems out of this world? Hold that thought. This Per-Capita Theory does seem out of this world to me. In reality we are becoming that advanced civilization we have been looking for in outer space. Only time will tell "If" we are not alone. Again, because we are planning and activating international nuclear disarmament programs today, our advanced civilization should have many millenniums to continue developing economic stability and balance.

Last question: "What do the Red and Blue argue about most of the time?" Answer: money, health, education and tragedies.

Yes, immigration concerns and futurist wars remain legitimate concerns within Per-Capita Theory advancement.

The Per-Capita Theory

By S. N. Webster
DOB: 08/06/1946 – Boston
March 28, 2014

The forthcoming is portrayed in a lump-sum USA National Debt payment factor with an international per-capita; per their national treasure, balancing Foreign Per-Capita Economic Growth with ours.

All United States Foreign Loans extended over the last decades will be repaid here-in.

The basic objective is to employ overpopulation with-in the prayer that we overcome Eternal War.

Again the basic objective is to add an economic growth factor that does NOT take from the rich to give to the poor as its primary function.

The human factor is both primary and obligatory with-in the separation of powers honored with my home the USA.
Here-with. no country is left behind.

The Per-Capita Theory:
Portrayed in a lump-sum USA National Debt Payment Factor,
with Per-Capita Economic Growth

The following is a U. S. National Debt lump-sum payment plan.
By: S. N. Webster, DOB: 08/06/46, Boston

July 18th, 2012

Country	Population Est. within 4-years	Amount of economic fluid cash growth. Primary non-TAX based economic growth, NO- Interest and no 1st TAX.
USA	313,012,264	$16-Trillion: National Debt only. $20-Trillion; Payment with $4-Tril back-up

Taxes vs. NATO / U.N. Growth on a USA National Debt Payment Plan

There is a big difference between a $20-Trillion tax-based loan with interest and the program here-in briefed. The Per-Capita Theory is up-front economic growth. This is a Treasury based growth process without a national tax-based pay-back of the whole capitol amount or any smaller part. Again the intellectual and moral interest is secured with political oversight within the democratic process word-wide.

Grow as an economic democracy because our republic requires the economic support. The world needs economic support. The EURO needs the same internal economic support. Growing as an economic democracy; here-in, can lead the world to stability. Every participating country in the FREE World has to be responsible and transparent with their national advance based on trust, balance, and oversight by a well educated public.

I submit that the issue in the English language has been tabled and ask for further elaboration and cultural adaptability be applied in appropriate languages.

Per Capita Theory

Country	Population Est., Within 4-years	Amount of economic fluid cash. National Economic Growth that must remain internally consumed by citizens there-of.

USA population 313,012,264 divided into $16-Trillion = Appox. $50,500.00
Our U. S. Per-Capita National Standard would be $50,500.00
NATO and Free World would apply our National Standard to their
population then into their National Treasury one country at a time.
Here-in the USA would participate as an equal recipient, even a second time.

#1: Albania   3,195,000 x $50,500.00 x International Exchange = $
#2: Belgium   10,839,905 x $50,500.00 x International Exchange = $
#3: Bulgaria   7,351,234 x $50,500.00 x International Exchange = $
#4: Canada   34,493,000 x $50,500.00 x International Exchange = $
#5: Croatia   4,425,747 x $50,500.00 x International Exchange = $
#6: Check Rep   10,549,100 x $50,500.00 x International Exchange = $
#7: Denmark   5,560,628 x $50,500.00 x International Exchange = $
#8: Estonia   1,340,122 x $50,500.00 x International Exchange = $
#9: France   65,821,885 x $50,500.00 x International Exchange = $
#10: Germany   81,802,000
#11: Greece   11,306,183   Doing the math is not easy.
#12: Hungary   10,014,324
#13: Iceland   318,452   The amount of economic support
#14: Italy   60,626,183   to NATO and the Free World is
#15: Latvia   2,221,100   staggering. As an engineer you know
#16: Lithuania   1,225,300   that the critical material used equals
#17: Luxembourg   502,100   the stability of the building project.
#18: Netherlands   16,677,300
#19: Norway   4,920,305
#20: Poland   38,482,919
#21: Portugal   10,636,888
#22: Romania   21,466,174   This is the question. Do you want to
#23: Slovakia   5,435,273   end our United States National Debt?
#24: Slovenia   2,052,130
#25: Spain   46,148,605   Be part of the solution.
#26: Turkey   73,722,988

Free World, only some of the free world countries are represented on/in this brief simply to shorten the subject to a brief.

#27: United Kingdom 62,006,048 x $50,000.00 x International Exchange =
#28: United States   311,610,000 The USA pays off her debt & rides free.
#29: Afghanistan   30,000,000 x $50,500.00 x International Exchange = $
#30: Bangladesh   150,782,000 x $50,500.00 x International Exchange = $
#31: Brazil   190,732694 x $50,500.00 x International Exchange = $
#32: Egypt   80,423,000
#33: Ethiopia   79,455,634
#34: India   1,210,193,422   Doing the math is not easy.
#35: Indonesia   237,556,363   Doing the math is worth it.
#36: Iran   75,639,000   Doing the math takes a team.
#37: Iraq   31,672,000
#38: Japan   127,950,000   Again, the economic support to
#39: Jordan   4,200,000   NATO and the Free World is
#40: Mexico   112,336,538   staggering.
#41: Pakistan   176,419,000
#42: Philippines   94,013,200   The USA is a NATO member.
#43: Republic of China 1,339,742,852
#44: Rep of Congo   65,966,000   Help the USA pay her
#45: Republic of Georgia   5,500,000   National Debt, today
#46: Russia   142,905,000   without borrowing the
#47: S. Africa   48,981,300   revenue.
#48: S. Korea   48,988,833
#49: Vietnam   87,375,000   Be part of the solution !

White Collar fraud, corruption, and misuse of the funds would become a stepped-up international security force issue innately financed with-in the growth policy itself; another secret service and another visible armed enforcement team joining existing national security forces.

In review:

The purpose of this plan is to pay off our US National Debt in lump-sum fassion and economically refortify NATO, her countries, her peoples, and the Free World; to refortify our very own United States of America.

How did we get here? You and I got here trying to pay off a growing National debt while embracing full employment. The last time we saw our country this divided and torn was during the United States Civil War.

Grow as an economic democracy because our republic needs the financial support and moral leadership. The here-in Per-Capita Theory of economic expansion envelopes the 22nd Century; logically embracing technologically enhanced employment and technologically enhanced education that cost more than the product while supporting the full employment goals of local areas in the poorest and the wealthiest areas in our nation.

In the beginning of this Per-Capita Theory as in the duration of advancement; the more the USA accepts to use the more the world gets to use in following the United States economic advancement via Per-Capita Theory.

Respectfully your in Christ @ Sea & @ Home.

With Peace of Mind.

____

S. N. Webster

Per-Capita Theory - Page #4 of 4

A letter to
NATO

S.N. Webster
DOB: 08/06/46, Boston

The Nuclear Age

NATO: NO-Nuclear First Strike Strategy.

September 1st. 2012 Iran just signed a Scientific and Technological Compact to be a team against the USA and Western World. Today the USA and the Western World hold a true NO-Nuclear First Strike Strategy with-in a nuclear stock-pile reduction in active procedure. By North Korea and Iran forming a pact to not participate in Peacemaking with NATO, NATO stands aware of this Iran and North Korea Compact to be a team. in an effort to communicate something before all parties present: NATO being many.

There was struggle on the ground when the Ayatollah Khomeini over-threw the Shaw of Iran. There was struggle on the ground when the Berlin Wall fell. There was struggle on the ground when Communism fell. There was struggle on the ground when Sadam fell. There was struggle on the ground when Osama bin Laden fell. Now while both Iran and North Korea propose themselves a targeted team. With the destruction of large cities and large industrial areas ominous, NATO must keep communications open. NATO must consider this Iran and North Korea Compact a threat to NATO security. NATO must ask: What is the missing objective; something thousands of years old, hundreds of years old or something contemporary? The solution is contemporary. The solution may seem to take forever. The solution is our standard.

Free Agent: SNW

Presented to: 23rd December 2009
Secretary of Defense Dr. Robert M. Gates
Room 3D 852   Free Agent SNW
2600 Defense/Pentagon   S. N. Webster
Alexandria, Virginia 20301-2600   Juno Beach, Florida

Presentation Title:

Appomattox vs. Armageddon
2010 – 2020

"A No First Nuclear Strike Strategy"
with-in the
"Tilted Ring Halo of Saturn Mission"
As described here-in to Senator Bill Nelson, Nov. 18, 2009

Submitted by: S.N. Webster, Free Agent SNW

Proposed for Development and Deployment:

Proposed Recipients of Developed/Accepted Mission Objective:
  Kim Long, as with the People of North Korea
  Osama bin Laden, as with the People of Afghanistan and Turkey
  President Abasidad, as with the People of Iran
  President Chavez, as with the People of Venezuela
  All Anti-USA and Anti-Israeli Radical Military Forces
  All of the United States and all Allied Countries/Nations

Free Agent SNW, 23/Dec/2009

United States Department of Defense   23rd December 2009
Secretary of Defense, Dr. Robert M. Gates
Room 3D 852   Free Agent SNW
2600 Defense /Pentagon   S.N. Webster
Alexandria, Virginia 20301-2600   Juno Beach, Florida

Reference: Title – **Appomattox vs. Armageddon**
                    "A Nuclear Disarmament Dialogue"
Time Window: 10-Years to focus date of 2020
Attached: 5-Page letter to Senator Bill Nelson; 18/11/09
                    3-Page letter to U.S. President Obama 02/02/09
Presenter: Free Agent SNW, Unlicensed

Dear Dr. Secretary Robert M. Gates,

Sir, I am Steven Nichols Webster; Free Agent SNW Unlicensed, born in Boston on 08/06/1946. I reside on 351 Zenith Lane, Juno Beach, Florida in Palm Beach County just south of Jupiter, Florida just southeast of US Hwy #1 and Donald Ross off Ocean Blvd. Cancers have taken me from the Sea and my life as a merchant officer. However I remain and in explanation of this focus date of 2020 I recall a voyage into the Red Sea.

My ship was the SS Coastal Corpus Christi. She was moored and back-loading wheat to and alongside the Greek vessel Golden Eye. It was back in 2000 in the Red Sea Port of Al Aquba, Jordon. We had delivered a world community cargo of wheat to Jordan. One of our Jordanian security guards; My guide went to great ends to explain the following as we eat dinner on our coiled bow mooring lines. My guide pleaded with me to understand and remember that it is written in and taught locally of the Koran that in the year 2020 all muslins of age will be motivated to take up stones and whatever means to march against Israel. He went on to say that most of the shore crew were college educated under Muslim Teachings of the Koran. All of the shore crew were very friendly and none held the same overbearing need to confront the 2020 issue. Sir, I have not studied the Koran nor can I validate this date of interest as an actual Koran reading.

In fact I can only retell what was told to me as a truth. There-in it is the opinion of this Free Agent SNW that an advanced study by appropriate personnel under your dispatch could verify this 2020 date issue and evaluate the probability that the Iranian Nuclear Missile Programs and Iranian Uranium Enrichment Programs are or are not seeking completion under the same 2020 time window.

Sir, this Koran passage is the only time window I will reference. The Israeli, Arab, and Muslim worlds have been of great interest to the US and our allies well before I was born. In so much as I feel that I would die before my time of fear, if fear kept me from presenting this time window to our Department of Defense foretelling a focus date of 2020 for Muslim hostilities to grow against Israel. If only a story Sir, thank you for listening to my story of the SS Coastal Corpus Christi in Al Aqaba, Jordan in the year 2000 under the Command of Captain Douglas Brown.

Issue: 2020 Time Window Closed.

Opening Issue: North Korean-Iranian "Backdoor to History".

A future without the North Korean and Iranian factors entering nuclear warfare capability is worth an

Appomattox vs. Armageddon

                                                          reality promoted today.

I have heard public radio announcements of untitled efforts by the US to offer the remaining Al Qaeda Fighters a way out of eternal battle with honor. Therefore I know the process is underway.

Focusing this **Appomattox vs. Armageddon** to an internal problem overcome within the USA will ease the international tension and open a **"Backdoor to History"** the United States of America can show the healing proof there-of as courage stands together today from both sides of our American Civil War. The American Civil War of 1861-1865 will hold the scales of justice in favor of ending nuclear proliferation for developing countries, races, and or religions.

There-in it is the opinion of this Free Agent that, North Korea is weighing in heavily on the Anti USA interests of Iran and holds no interest in Anti Israel fronts. It is also the opinion of this Free Agent SNW that North Korea will address interest in President Chavez's animosity against the United States. It is the opinion of this Free Agent SNW that the North Korean Submarine Fleet will boldly go forward where ordered. During a time of submarine hostilities the surrender alternative will be accepted in any port world wide. There-in the entire targeted nation/state could continue the Non-Proliferation of Nuclear and Advanced Weaponry Treaty.

Non-Proliferation of Nuclear Weaponry is security. I applaud the Pentagon's steadfast harbor in the **"No Nuclear First Strike"** loyalty in the face of other nation/state defiance and deception.

Having stood the **North Korean Nuclear Disarmament** agenda as a priority I must concede disappointment. I concede disappointment on my part; in my planning, in my announced belief that Kim Long would gladly accept discussing the option of "Financial Government Based Growth with an attached Non-Proliferation of Nuclear Weaponry" <u>over the right</u> for independent countries to grow independently in what ever direction they want to reach towards. From my letter to Senator Bill Nelson I draw faith that North Korea will peacefully partake in the victory feast of Nuclear Nations with Non-Proliferation of Warhead Programs.

The dialogue I represent is not of standard protocol. The dialogue I represent is of a Counter Intelligence type; presented in expectation of humanizing the independence of opposing political entities in order that we achieve nuclear disarmament among all nations be they Communist, Socialist, Capitalist, Muslim, Christian, Hindu, Secular, etc., etc.

Sir, I am in a weakened state of health at present with lymphoma and cancer. My priorities are to save lives. Our United States of America All Volunteer Armed Forces has proven that our spirit can bridge race, religion, and politics. In the 60's and 70's we chose to enter Beijing; not by bayonets and bullets under the status quo of Western Expansionism. We chose to enter Beijing by an untested economic industrial partnership with China. Our All Volunteer Armed Forces was enacted in tribute to that change in political direction. We are now in Recession over that Economic Experiment and an internal rebellion backed by inflation based financial structure collapses. We are not a 1st Strike Nuclear Strategist Nation holding a Nuclear Disarmament Time Table.

We; the USA, are opening several internal economic expansion policies that will help to find international partnership there-in.

If I can use humor to change Kim Long's attitude into honoring the Nuclear Disarmament proceeding of today I will save generations the pain, suffering, and the tension of a divided world. If you approve my approach during the existing countdown in strategies my life's work will be tested. I do humbly seek a normal low level paid position while formally writing a transitional strategy follow up of human interaction carried on by official and professional statesmen, diplomats of President Obama's choice and military attaches of your choice. I am but a minority. I am simply a Christian minority with an attitude and life experience of my own.

Dr. Secretary of Defense Sir, I hold you and the men and woman of our All Volunteer Armed Forces in the highest esteem among the most elite circles on Earth.

In Closing Sir: The dialogue I would use to convince an active anti-USA and/or anti non-proliferation of nuclear warhead protagonist nation/state would be of a Counter Intelligence type such as: "In WW1 and WW2 the Germans said: If the Americans can fight the French and English so can we." Today the EU has combined those European Nations under the EURO; nations that have known a history explained by the wars between themselves since their beginning, those nations are doing all that is possible to out-smart that age-old "war to advancement mentality".

Attached: 1-Page, Classified Technology; verb & noun only.

Merry Christmas and Peace on Earth, Sir.

Respectfully yours in Christ @ Sea & @ Home.

____

Steven Nichols Webster
Free Agent SNW

SN Webster, 351 Zenith Lane, Juno Beach, Florida, 33408
Contact: 561-568-3265   E-mail: snwebster@earthlink.net

Listen up !

No
Monkey Business
In the
Wheelhouse

Ok !

That also means no food or drinks on the chart table.
No food or drinks of any kind on or near electronics.

Anyone with children, these last pages are for you.
Here is the beginning of our Great Circle Study

Dear Pre-Readers,

The audible joy of being read to has
been known for millenniums.
A millennium is 1,000 years.
A century is 100 years.
A decade is 10 years.
And, how old are you ?
I am _____ years old.
My name is _____________________.

You that can read, read to a pre-reader.
Read to a pre-reader as a big brother.
Read to a pre-reader as a big sister.
Read to a pre-reader as a friend.

Welcome aboard !

The
Sea of Math

"Division"

An Introduction to Time and the four Directions
North, East, South, and West

Benchmarks Achieved

An Introduction to

"*Division*"

1/2s, 1/3s, 1/4s, 1/5s, & 1/6s

Grades: K – 3

Learning how to tell time.
How mathematical time came to be;
60 seconds a minute, 60 minutes an hour, 24 hours a day.

Learning our four directions; North, East, South, and West.
How the 360 Degrees of our compass
came to be.

*Our highest academic benchmark
achieved in this lesson is
Division.*

The ship sailed by students "The Sea of Math" is found on an
exterior wall of the Pagosa Springs Elementary School in
Archuleta County School District, Colorado.

This is a
Great Circle Study
By
Nick

First we are going to learn something about

Mathematical Compatibility.

*We will start by answering the question: Why do we have
12 hours, 60 minutes, and 60 seconds on the face of our clock?*

*We will then take this observation one step farther to answer the
question: Why do we have 360 degrees to our nautical compass?*

We will start with a circle.

Now, we divide that circle in half.

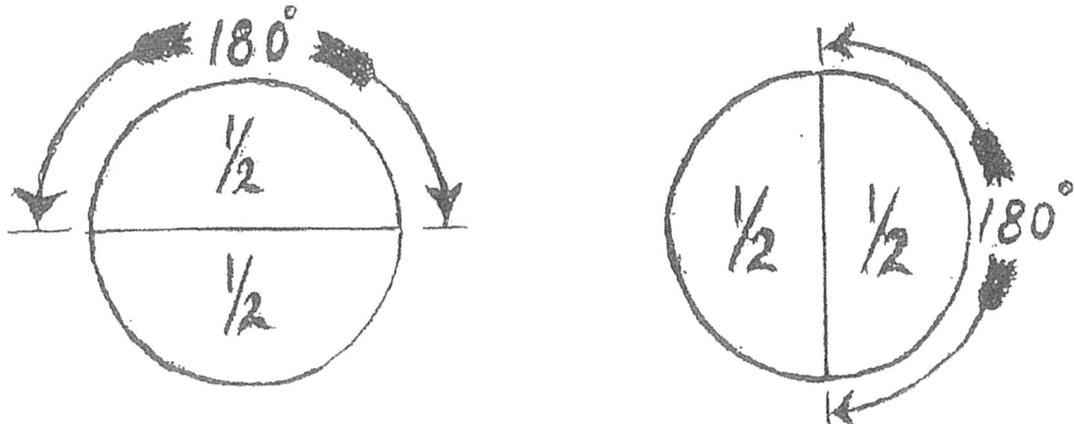

*One half of 360 is 180.
We already know there are 360 degrees in a circle.
We are about to learn why.*

Introduction Page #1

½ × ½ = ¼

One half of one half is one quarter.

One quarter of 360 is 90.

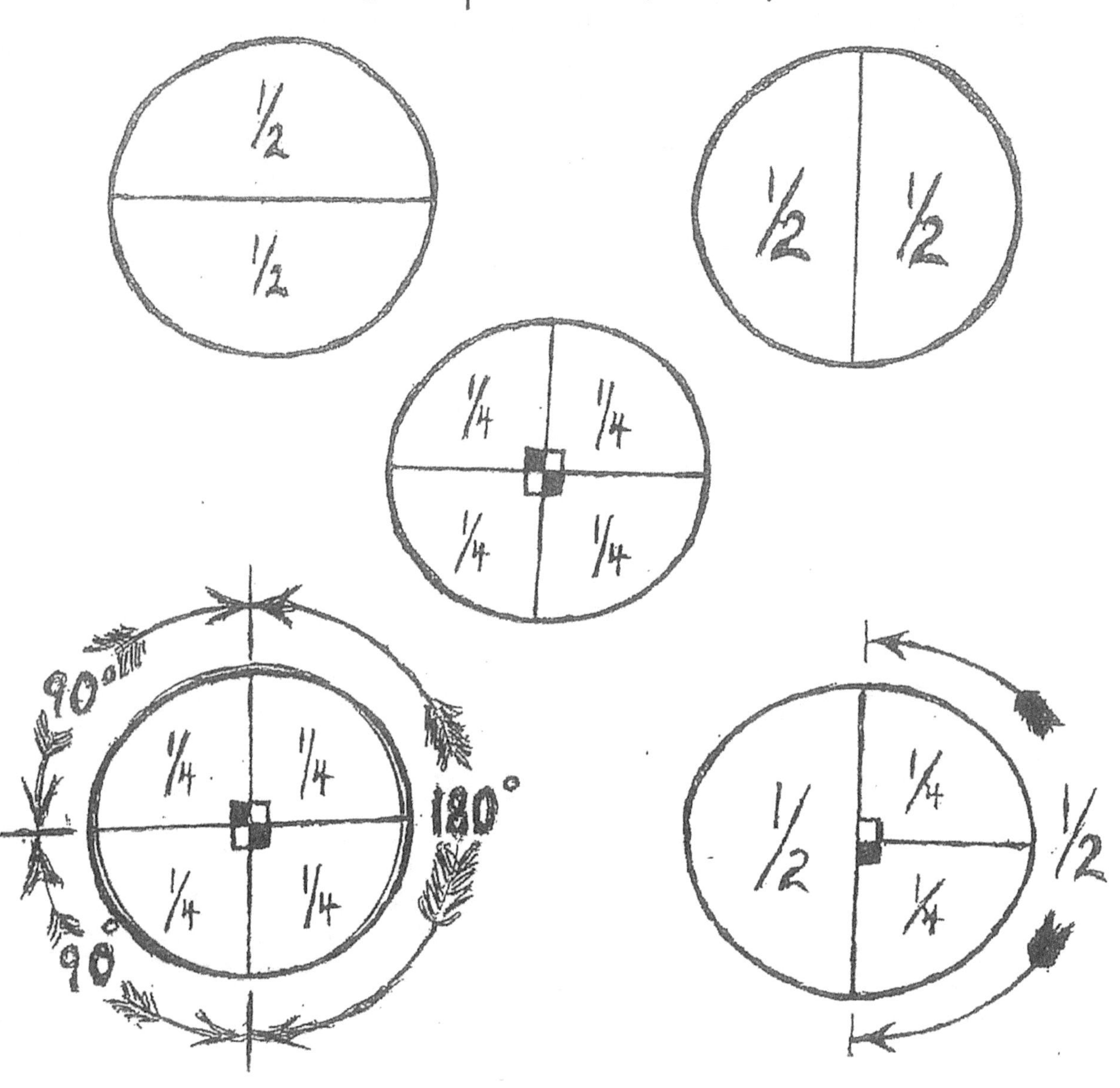

Introduction Page #2

1/3 x ¼ = 1/12

One third of one quarter equals one twelfth.
The 12 hours on the face of our clock.
The hour hand goes around twice for the
12 hours of day and 12 hours of night.

A. M. means At Morning.   P. M. means Past Morning

Midnight to Noon   Noon to Midnight

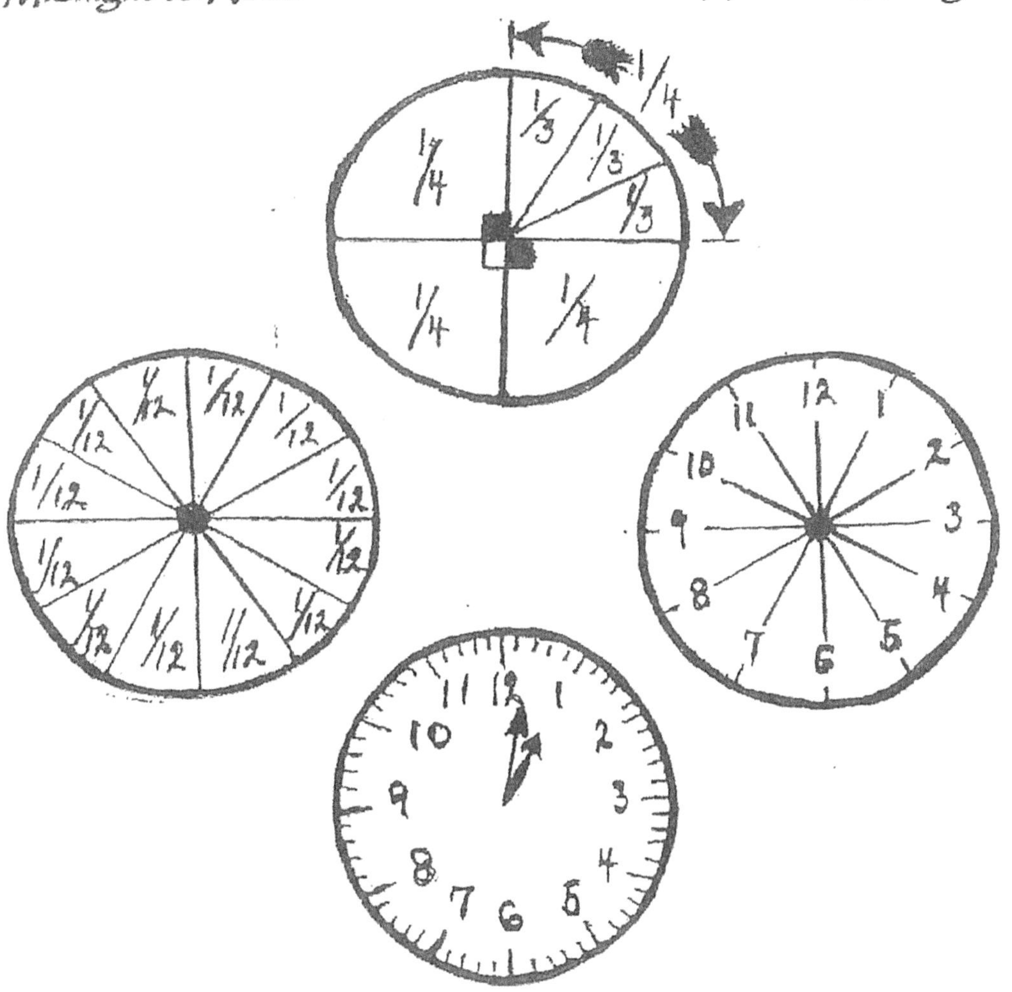

1/5 x 1/12 = 1/60

One fifth of one twelfth equals one sixtieth.
The 60 seconds of every minute and the 60 minutes of every hour.

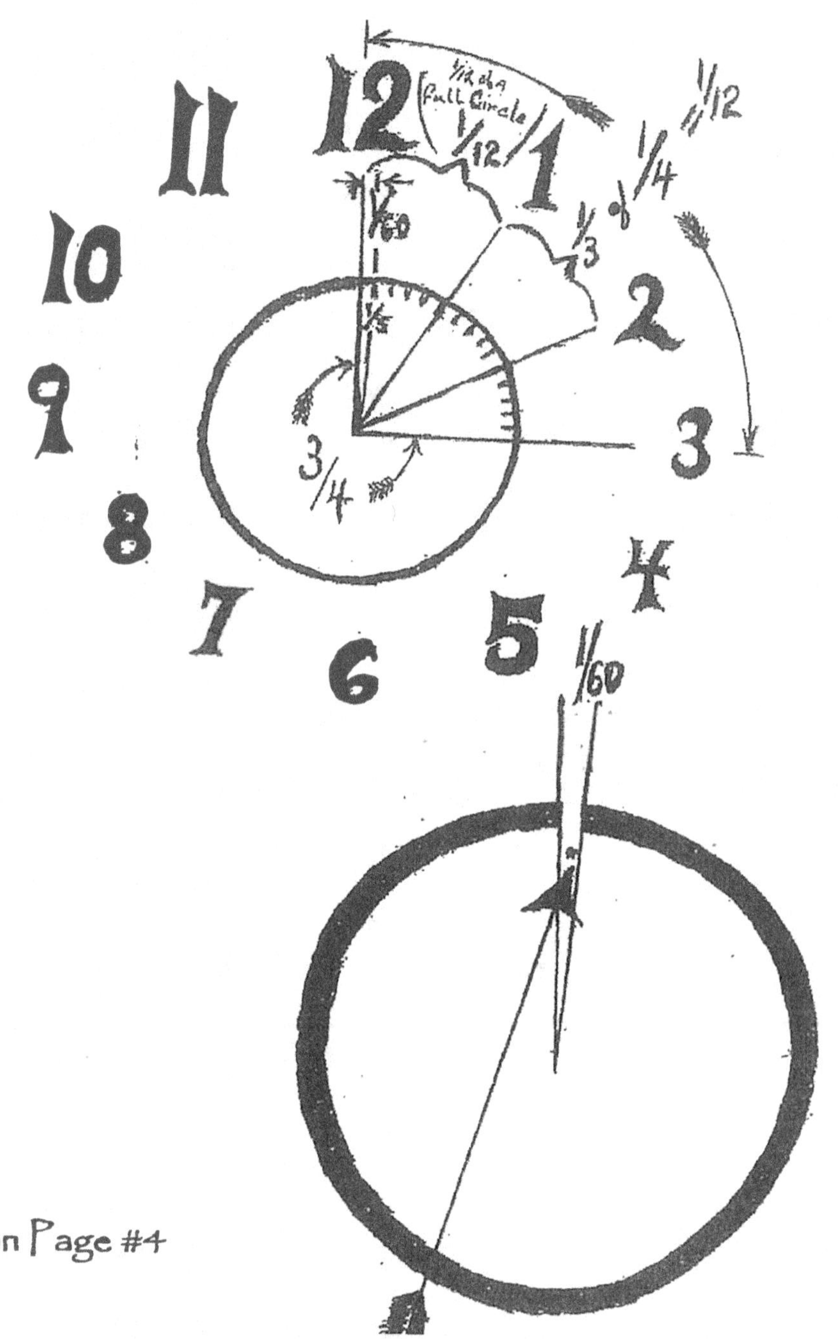

Introduction Page #4

1/6 x 1/60 = 1/360

One sixth of one sixtieth equals one three hundred sixtieth.
This gives us the 360 Degrees of our Nautical Compass.

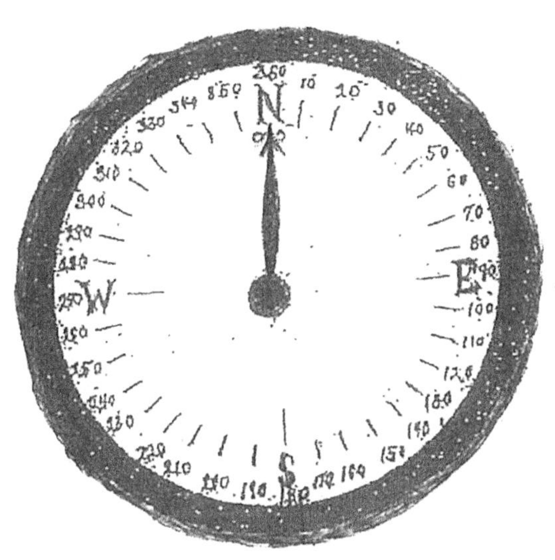

&

The 360 Degree CIRCLE

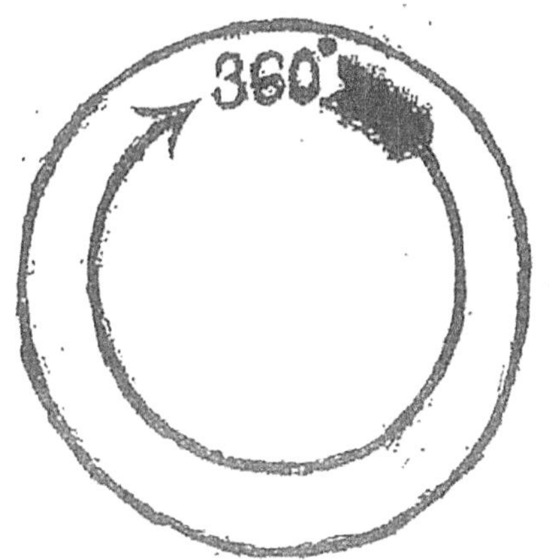

Introduction Page #5

Latitudes

Division

We divided a circle by 1/2.
The we divided that 1/2 into 1/4s.

That is how latitudes took form.

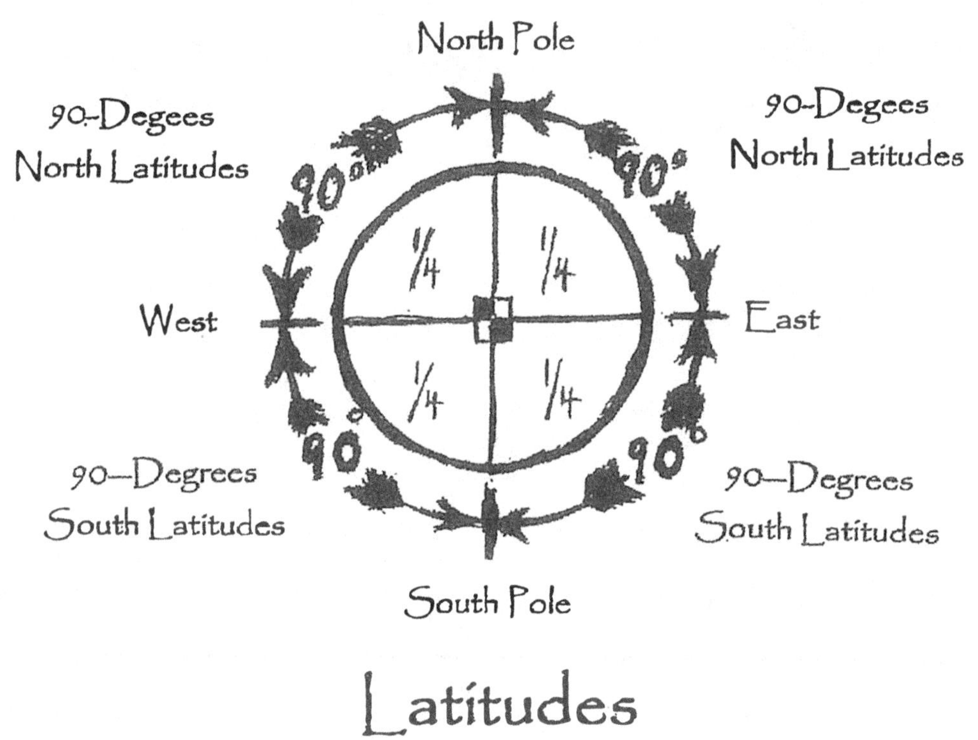

Latitudes

Introduction Page #6

Longitudes

Division

We divided a circle by 1/2.

That is how longitudes took form.

Longitudes

Introduction Page #7

Turtle Town Marina
Division
An Introduction to Fractions
1/2, 1/3, 1/4, 1/5, 1/6

Grades K-3

Student's Name: ___________________
Date: ___________________
Grade in school: _______
Pre-study test grade: ________
After-study test grade: _______

"1ˢᵗ Test"

#1: Each student will read aloud. To pass this test you must read the first 7 pages of this textbook aloud. Yes, you must read aloud to fellow students, an instructor, or to a parent.

Test Page #1

Credits:

I thank every teacher I have ever had.
I especially thank my first and second grade teachers;
Mrs. Warren and Mrs. Lawrence.

That was back in Topsfield, Massachusetts in the 1950's.

I remember asking myself, "Why?".

About the Author

Poetry and Politics

"The Sea; She"
"A Perfect Storm"
"Laughter and Failure"
"Failure and Laughter"
"The Red and the Blue"
"Fear and Hatred"

"The Sea; She."

The Sea; She.

The Sea; She of immortal soul.

The Sea; She beckons for my return.

The Sea; She is always the stronger and mightier than I.

The Sea; She always holds me as if her babe in cradle, in calm, and in storm.

The Sea; She holds her fair rules of passage in calm & in the reach of storm.

The Sea; She if I betray will send me to my mortal grave.

The Sea; She beckons for my return.

The Sea; She of immortal soul.

The Sea: She.

A Perfect Storm

With God's help we made it home through a Perfect Storm back in 1984. We; the **Becky M,** were returning to New Bedford, MA from a sword-fishing voyage in the Grand Banks of Newfoundland. That perfect storm headed east as we headed west. At the height of the storm we encountered six days of perfect 20-foot Seas. Perfect because for six days you could see each 20 foot wave unbroken from horizon to horizon. Yes, every wave encountered and the 5 or 6 waves behind it were seen unbroken from horizon to horizon; for 6 days. We; a 95-foot steel-hull, would climb and break through the crest of each wave as we met. Those waves were comfortably spaced some football fields apart. However one wave was much thicker. I was at the helm as the whitewash cleared from our bow windows, then our side windows, and then our stern windows were all within a wave. I put one foot up incase my forward window gave way. We had been swallowed. Soon I could see the oncoming star light sky on the other side of that wave as we passed through unscathed. God rest the souls of those whom have not returned to family and friends ashore. My logbook account was stolen in Destin, Florida or I would share more of the story. It will be found one day. I signed on as the cook and ball drop man. That November of 1984 I studied under Capt Zook in Morehead City, N. C. Thereafter I tested for my first USCG 100-Ton Captain's License. Thank you Captain Jim Zook. Thank you Captain Greg Musk and Captain Dave Greenhouse; both instructors at the Star Center, American Maritime Officers Union, in Dania Beach, Florida. AMO Star Center, thank you for sharing and training me on
Captain Nathaniel Bowditch: 1773-1835,
beyond my navigation dreams.
AMO: 954-920-3222

"Laughter and Failure"

On an otherwise normal afternoon in the late summer of 2013 both Saint Peter and Saint Paul told me; speaking at the same time: "Nick, do not worry. Somebody else is better than you at everything you do."

I was building a Club House for Maddy and Eric; my girlfriend Diane's grandkids. The front door was chest high from my point of view and by the kids' request. The floating dock just down the sloping lawn had been dismantled and now added fond memories and building materials to the clubhouse. The Acushnet River had left distinct river markings on its planks that now made up the club-house roof. Cleared trees served as the 4-corner beams. I was done. The clubhouse was done. I had put all my tools in the tool shed and locked her up. All was in good order. I looked up to the sky and I prayed to God saying: "Lord God I think I am worse off now than when I started the club-house earlier this summer." Have you ever heard thunder speak? You must remember; once, how you just trusted somebody's booming voice sometime somewhere. Well I earnestly did not laugh, I thought: "Yes Sir!" Then the clouds said clearly: "Do not worry somebody else did everything that had to be done." And I listened with up right attention. Then the thunder said: "You have never loved a woman in your entire life." "If you had loved a woman you would have loved her for your children as well." Every woman I had ever dated in high school, known in college, met around the world, and then every woman I had lived with, and every excuse I held for never marrying surfaced, spun, and resurfaced. Yes presently my entire life swirled before my inner soul. Failure had become obvious as I continually thought: "Yes Sir!" I had just survived bone and blood cancer. The chemo was over. It was my first free time in years. I spent the entire summer building that club-house for

Diane's grand-kids with all the strength I could muster. Just breathing made me happy. Now, I was frozen in my tracks. I knew I was listening to the rolling thunder and watching the forming clouds within a conversation with the sky. Then that distant thunder turned into laughter as Saint Peter and Saint Paul were laughing behind and with the clouds saying: "Nick, when have you ever been right." They were commenting about my thoughts. I mean I saw the sky open when Saint Peter and Saint Paul said; "Nick, in your entire life, when have you ever been right?" I was better off than I thought. As they laughed so uncontrollably they shared that joy of laughter with me. As they shared that joy, I felt better. After all I had come close to a state of shock. Then the storm clouds changed more normally into light rain over the neighborhood. I could see that "everybody else" the clouds were speaking of as my neighbors which did marry and have children of their own; my neighborhood. Balance of thought and deed returned to me as I could see the Bible phrase: "Love your neighbor as thyself". I continued to walk my way to the main house with a little haste before it rained. I do feel much better even unto today. Thinking again today about failure, I whole heartedly agree with Saint Peter and Saint Paul. I can not go back to then now. Now, I say: Amen !

"Smile" : I do need more than a hand full of aeronautical engineers etc. that are better than me at everything I do to fly our mission aircraft/spacecraft for Project: Good Karma "R&D" in all her glory.

"Failure and Laughter"

In 2002 I had third place in the high power nationals at Fort Clinton with two rounds to go. Failure; let me tell you about failure. The officials had changed the scoring range for a shared first, second, and third in 2002. That made it easier to go home with a medal. We were on a 100 yard open range using high power long guns. 98 rounds out of my 100 had me tied for third at the Nationals. Well; honest, I shot at the wrong target or missed my entire target for the first time during that last and final ten shots standing; the 99th shot. On my 100th shot I again missed my target. Most likely I aimed at somebody else's target. My last two bullets; at the peak of need and concentration, are such small things in reality. Let us say four inches each. Oh, I made it a mountain. It was my life or death moment. As it was I scored something about 35th to 16th from last in 2002. I got to feeling pretty normal after a year or so. Failure makes room for learning. Learning is a lifelong experience. Anybody ever ask you what failure is? I am much happier now having made more room for learning.

We now turn to Nick Webster's "Political View of the Red and Blue"

I, Nick Webster, serve both God and Country in my political writings. This binding of subject matter creates a political Double Agent standard. Here-in is my "Official" opinion of our USA as is. Our USA today is almost perfect. I see not opposition but opportunity. I see a more perfect union on the way. Our USA will face all obstacles present and future times may bring; we will face them with many hands, hearts, and minds working together. God bless our USA.

"Fear and Hatred"

I am your local Hans Solo; hard-at-work.
You have read about my NASA project "Good Karma".
I am presently serving a lifetime sentence for an act
I am truly innocent there-of.
This is a true story.

My name is Steven Nichols Webster; "Captain Nick",
DOB: 08/06/1946; Boston
Free Agent SNW - Licensed

Today I live on 400 Money Island Drive in Atlantic Beach, North
Carolina, 28512. I passed my second DUI/DWI breath test in
Baldwin County, Alabama some years ago.
I had drunk only one beer in 24 hours that day some years ago.
I logically passed the breath test and was still convicted.
I have no accidents. I caused no injuries. I caused no property damage.
I have no associated tickets with any DUI/DWI.
During my last and 4th DUI Deputy Ken Christmas changed the arrest
site from the USCG Auxiliary drive-way by East Pass Bridge
to Brooks Bridge on the opposite end of
Okaloosa Island, Florida.
That is the truth and the reason
I have a lifetime sentence never to drive again.
I hurt nobody nor did I damage any property ever.
Yes, I have a Lifetime DMV Driver's License Suspension.
I contest my lifetime driver's license suspension.
What produced that unbalanced judgment?

Credits

<u>Our United States Armed Forces</u>

United States Army
United States Navy
United States Marines
United States Air Force
United States Coast Guard
United States Merchant Marines

Thank You
NASA

Thank you "One and All" for your service.

Thank you:
RTM Star Center
American Maritime Officer's Union
2 West Dixie Highway, Dania Beach, Florida 33408
My last employer

Thank you
Family, Friends, and Neighbors.

North Carolina
First in Flight
1903

Project: "Good Karma"
2017